(Amd)

MENACHEM BEGIN

MENACHEM BEGIN

Richard Amdur

CHELSEA HOUSE PUBLISHERS
NEW YORK
PHILADELPHIA

EDITOR-IN-CHIEF: Nancy Toff
EXECUTIVE EDITOR: Remmel T. Nunn
MANAGING EDITOR: Karyn Gullen Browne
COPY CHIEF: Juliann Barbato
PICTURE EDITOR: Adrian G. Allen
ART DIRECTOR: Giannella Garrett
MANUFACTURING MANAGER: Gerald Levine

Staff for MENACHEM BEGIN:

SENIOR EDITOR: John W. Selfridge
ASSISTANT EDITORS: Pierre Hauser, Kathleen McDermott, Bert Yaeger
EDITORIAL ASSISTANT: James Guiry
COPY EDITORS: Gillian Bucky, Sean Dolan, Michael Goodman, Ellen Scordato
ASSOCIATE PICTURE EDITOR: Juliette Dickstein
SENIOR DESIGNER: Debby Jay
ASSISTANT DESIGNER: Jill Goldreyer
DESIGNERS: Laura Lang, Donna Sinisgalli
PICTURE RESEARCH: Cheryl Moch
PRODUCTION COORDINATOR: Laura McCormick
COVER ILLUSTRATION: Neil Waldman

CREATIVE DIRECTOR: Harold Steinberg

Frontispiece courtesy of Israeli Consulate General Library

3 5 7 9 8 6 4

Library of Congress Cataloging in Publication Data

Amdur, Richard. MENACHEM BEGIN

(World leaders past & present)
Bibliography: p.
Includes index.
1. Begin, Menachem, 1913–   —Juvenile literature. 2.
Prime ministers—Israel—Biography—Juvenile literature.
3. Revisionist Zionists—Poland—Biography—Juvenile
literature. 4. Israel—Politics and government—Juvenile
literature. [1. Begin, Menachem, 1913–   . 2. Prime
ministers] I. Title. II. Series.
DS126.6.B33A53   1988   956.94′054′0924 [B]
[92] 87-15093

ISBN 0-87754-561-8
      0-7910-0556-9 (pbk.)

Contents

WORLD LEADERS PAST & PRESENT

John Adams
John Quincy Adams
Konrad Adenauer
Alexander the Great
Salvador Allende
Marc Antony
Corazon Aquino
Yasir Arafat
King Arthur
Hafez al-Assad
Kemal Atatürk
Attila
Clement Attlee
Augustus Caesar
Menachem Begin
David Ben-Gurion
Otto von Bismarck
Léon Blum
Simon Bolívar
Cesare Borgia
Willy Brandt
Leonid Brezhnev
Julius Caesar
John Calvin
Jimmy Carter
Fidel Castro
Catherine the Great
Charlemagne
Chiang Kai-Shek
Winston Churchill
Georges Clemenceau
Cleopatra
Constantine the Great
Hernán Cortés
Oliver Cromwell
Georges-Jacques
  Danton
Jefferson Davis
Moshe Dayan
Charles de Gaulle
Eamon De Valera
Eugene Debs
Deng Xiaoping
Benjamin Disraeli
Alexander Dubček
François & Jean-Claude
  Duvalier
Dwight Eisenhower
Eleanor of Aquitaine
Elizabeth i
Faisal
Ferdinand & Isabella
Francisco Franco
Benjamin Franklin

Frederick the Great
Indira Gandhi
Mohandas Gandhi
Giuseppe Garibaldi
Amin & Bashir Gemayel
Genghis Khan
William Gladstone
Mikhail Gorbachev
Ulysses S. Grant
Ernesto "Che" Guevara
Tenzin Gyatso
Alexander Hamilton
Dag Hammarskjöld
Henry viii
Henry of Navarre
Paul von Hindenburg
Hirohito
Adolf Hitler
Ho Chi Minh
King Hussein
Ivan the Terrible
Andrew Jackson
James i
Wojciech Jaruzelski
Thomas Jefferson
Joan of Arc
Pope John xxiii
Pope John Paul ii
Lyndon Johnson
Benito Juárez
John Kennedy
Robert Kennedy
Jomo Kenyatta
Ayatollah Khomeini
Nikita Khrushchev
Kim Il Sung
Martin Luther King, Jr.
Henry Kissinger
Kublai Khan
Lafayette
Robert E. Lee
Vladimir Lenin
Abraham Lincoln
David Lloyd George
Louis xiv
Martin Luther
Judas Maccabeus
James Madison
Nelson & Winnie
  Mandela
Mao Zedong
Ferdinand Marcos
George Marshall

Mary, Queen of Scots
Tomáš Masaryk
Golda Meir
Klemens von Metternich
James Monroe
Hosni Mubarak
Robert Mugabe
Benito Mussolini
Napoléon Bonaparte
Gamal Abdel Nasser
Jawaharlal Nehru
Nero
Nicholas ii
Richard Nixon
Kwame Nkrumah
Daniel Ortega
Mohammed Reza Pahlavi
Thomas Paine
Charles Stewart
  Parnell
Pericles
Juan Perón
Peter the Great
Pol Pot
Muammar el-Qaddafi
Ronald Reagan
Cardinal Richelieu
Maximilien Robespierre
Eleanor Roosevelt
Franklin Roosevelt
Theodore Roosevelt
Anwar Sadat
Haile Selassie
Prince Sihanouk
Jan Smuts
Joseph Stalin
Sukarno
Sun Yat-sen
Tamerlane
Mother Teresa
Margaret Thatcher
Josip Broz Tito
Toussaint L'Ouverture
Leon Trotsky
Pierre Trudeau
Harry Truman
Queen Victoria
Lech Walesa
George Washington
Chaim Weizmann
Woodrow Wilson
Xerxes
Emiliano Zapata
Zhou Enlai

CHELSEA HOUSE PUBLISHERS

ON LEADERSHIP
Arthur M. Schlesinger, jr.

LEADERSHIP, it may be said, is really what makes the world go round. Love no doubt smooths the passage; but love is a private transaction between consenting adults. Leadership is a public transaction with history. The idea of leadership affirms the capacity of individuals to move, inspire, and mobilize masses of people so that they act together in pursuit of an end. Sometimes leadership serves good purposes, sometimes bad; but whether the end is benign or evil, great leaders are those men and women who leave their personal stamp on history.

Now, the very concept of leadership implies the proposition that individuals can make a difference. This proposition has never been universally accepted. From classical times to the present day, eminent thinkers have regarded individuals as no more than the agents and pawns of larger forces, whether the gods and goddesses of the ancient world or, in the modern era, race, class, nation, the dialectic, the will of the people, the spirit of the times, history itself. Against such forces, the individual dwindles into insignificance.

So contends the thesis of historical determinism. Tolstoy's great novel *War and Peace* offers a famous statement of the case. Why, Tolstoy asked, did millions of men in the Napoleonic wars, denying their human feelings and their common sense, move back and forth across Europe slaughtering their fellows? "The war," Tolstoy answered, "was bound to happen simply because it was bound to happen." All prior history predetermined it. As for leaders, they, Tolstoy said, "are but the labels that serve to give a name to an end and, like labels, they have the least possible connection with the event." The greater the leader, "the more conspicuous the inevitability and the predestination of every act he commits." The leader, said Tolstoy, is "the slave of history."

Determinism takes many forms. Marxism is the determinism of class. Nazism the determinism of race. But the idea of men and women as the slaves of history runs athwart the deepest human instincts. Rigid determinism abolishes the idea of human freedom—

the assumption of free choice that underlies every move we make, every word we speak, every thought we think. It abolishes the idea of human responsibility, since it is manifestly unfair to reward or punish people for actions that are by definition beyond their control. No one can live consistently by any deterministic creed. The Marxist states prove this themselves by their extreme susceptibility to the cult of leadership.

More than that, history refutes the idea that individuals make no difference. In December 1931 a British politician crossing Park Avenue in New York City between 76th and 77th Streets around 10:30 P.M. looked in the wrong direction and was knocked down by an automobile—a moment, he later recalled, of a man aghast, a world aglare: "I do not understand why I was not broken like an eggshell or squashed like a gooseberry." Fourteen months later an American politician, sitting in an open car in Miami, Florida, was fired on by an assassin; the man beside him was hit. Those who believe that individuals make no difference to history might well ponder whether the next two decades would have been the same had Mario Constasino's car killed Winston Churchill in 1931 and Giuseppe Zangara's bullet killed Franklin Roosevelt in 1933. Suppose, in addition, that Adolf Hitler had been killed in the street fighting during the Munich *Putsch* of 1923 and that Lenin had died of typhus during World War I. What would the 20th century be like now?

For better or for worse, individuals do make a difference. "The notion that a people can run itself and its affairs anonymously," wrote the philosopher William James, "is now well known to be the silliest of absurdities. Mankind does nothing save through initiatives on the part of inventors, great or small, and imitation by the rest of us—these are the sole factors in human progress. Individuals of genius show the way, and set the patterns, which common people then adopt and follow."

Leadership, James suggests, means leadership in thought as well as in action. In the long run, leaders in thought may well make the greater difference to the world. But, as Woodrow Wilson once said, "Those only are leaders of men, in the general eye, who lead in action. . . . It is at their hands that new thought gets its translation into the crude language of deeds." Leaders in thought often invent in solitude and obscurity, leaving to later generations the tasks of imitation. Leaders in action—the leaders portrayed in this series—have to be effective in their own time.

And they cannot be effective by themselves. They must act in response to the rhythms of their age. Their genius must be adapted, in a phrase of William James's, "to the receptivities of the moment." Leaders are useless without followers. "There goes the mob," said the French politician hearing a clamor in the streets. "I am their leader. I must follow them." Great leaders turn the inchoate emotions of the mob to purposes of their own. They seize on the opportunities of their time, the hopes, fears, frustrations, crises, potentialities. They succeed when events have prepared the way for them, when the community is awaiting to be aroused, when they can provide the clarifying and organizing ideas. Leadership ignites the circuit between the individual and the mass and thereby alters history.

It may alter history for better or for worse. Leaders have been responsible for the most extravagant follies and most monstrous crimes that have beset suffering humanity. They have also been vital in such gains as humanity has made in individual freedom, religious and racial tolerance, social justice and respect for human rights.

There is no sure way to tell in advance who is going to lead for good and who for evil. But a glance at the gallery of men and women in *World Leaders—Past and Present* suggests some useful tests.

One test is this: do leaders lead by force or by persuasion? By command or by consent? Through most of history leadership was exercised by the divine right of authority. The duty of followers was to defer and to obey. "Theirs not to reason why,/ Theirs but to do and die." On occasion, as with the so-called "enlightened despots" of the 18th century in Europe, absolutist leadership was animated by humane purposes. More often, absolutism nourished the passion for domination, land, gold and conquest and resulted in tyranny.

The great revolution of modern times has been the revolution of equality. The idea that all people should be equal in their legal condition has undermined the old structure of authority, hierarchy and deference. The revolution of equality has had two contrary effects on the nature of leadership. For equality, as Alexis de Tocqueville pointed out in his great study *Democracy in America,* might mean equality in servitude as well as equality in freedom.

"I know of only two methods of establishing equality in the political world," Tocqueville wrote. "Rights must be given to every citizen, or none at all to anyone . . . save one, who is the master of all." There was no middle ground "between the sovereignty of all and the absolute power of one man." In his astonishing prediction of 20th-century totalitarian dictatorship, Tocqueville explained how the revolution of equality could lead to the *"Führerprinzip"* and more terrible absolutism than the world had ever known.

But when rights are given to every citizen and the sovereignty of all is established, the problem of leadership takes a new form, becomes more exacting than ever before. It is easy to issue commands and enforce them by the rope and the stake, the concentration camp and the *gulag.* It is much harder to use argument and achievement to overcome opposition and win consent. The Founding Fathers of the United States understood the difficulty. They believed that history had given them the opportunity to decide, as Alexander Hamilton wrote in the first Federalist Paper, whether men are indeed capable of basing government on "reflection and choice, or whether they are forever destined to depend . . . on accident and force."

Government by reflection and choice called for a new style of leadership and a new quality of followership. It required leaders to be responsive to popular concerns, and it required followers to be active and informed participants in the process. Democracy does not eliminate emotion from politics; sometimes it fosters demagoguery; but it is confident that, as the greatest of democratic leaders put it, you cannot fool all of the people all of the time. It measures leadership by results and retires those who overreach or falter or fail.

It is true that in the long run despots are measured by results too. But they can postpone the day of judgment, sometimes indefinitely, and in the meantime they can do infinite harm. It is also true that democracy is no guarantee of virtue and intelligence in government, for the voice of the people is not necessarily the voice of God. But democracy, by assuring the right of opposition, offers built-in resistance to the evils inherent in absolutism. As the theologian Reinhold Niebuhr summed it up, "Man's capacity for justice makes democracy possible, but man's inclination to injustice makes democracy necessary."

A second test for leadership is the end for which power is sought. When leaders have as their goal the supremacy of a master race or the promotion of totalitarian revolution or the acquisition and exploitation of colonies or the protection of greed and privilege or the preservation of personal power, it is likely that their leadership will do little to advance the cause of humanity. When their goal is the abolition of slavery, the liberation of women, the enlargement of opportunity for the poor and powerless, the extension of equal rights to racial minorities, the defense of the freedoms of expression and opposition, it is likely that their leadership will increase the sum of human liberty and welfare.

Leaders have done great harm to the world. They have also conferred great benefits. You will find both sorts in this series. Even "good" leaders must be regarded with a certain wariness. Leaders are not demigods; they put on their trousers one leg after another just like ordinary mortals. No leader is infallible, and every leader needs to be reminded of this at regular intervals. Irreverence irritates leaders but is their salvation. Unquestioning submission corrupts leaders and demands followers. Making a cult of a leader is always a mistake. Fortunately hero worship generates its own antidote. "Every hero," said Emerson, "becomes a bore at last."

The signal benefit the great leaders confer is to embolden the rest of us to live according to our own best selves, to be active, insistent, and resolute in affirming our own sense of things. For great leaders attest to the reality of human freedom against the supposed inevitabilities of history. And they attest to the wisdom and power that may lie within the most unlikely of us, which is why Abraham Lincoln remains the supreme example of great leadership. A great leader, said Emerson, exhibits new possibilities to all humanity. "We feed on genius. . . . Great men exist that there may be greater men."

Great leaders, in short, justify themselves by emancipating and empowering their followers. So humanity struggles to master its destiny, remembering with Alexis de Tocqueville: "It is true that around every man a fatal circle is traced beyond which he cannot pass; but within the wide verge of that circle he is powerful and free; as it is with man, so with communities."

1

The Hawk on a Mission of Peace

March 26, 1979, was a cold, gray day in Washington, D.C., but the gloomy weather was in striking contrast to the joyous and momentous occasion at hand — the leaders of Egypt and Israel had come to the U.S. capital to sign an agreement ending nearly 31 years of hostility between their countries. The hope in almost everyone's mind was that the treaty between two of the world's most unyielding opponents would also lead to an overall peace settlement in the Middle East, which remains among the most violent and war-torn regions of the world.

U.S. president Jimmy Carter had painstakingly conducted the delicate negotiations that led to the agreement; he was host to the elaborate signing ceremonies and would sign the treaty as a witness. Several thousand people were crowded onto the White House lawn to watch the historic ceremony, and a worldwide audience estimated at 100 million people saw the event on television. Some of the dignitaries present said the gathering seemed almost like a political rally.

Representing the people of Egypt was the elegant, impeccably dressed President Anwar Sadat, who had launched a war against Israel just five and a

> *We have one wish in our hearts, one wish in our souls— to bring peace to our people.*
> —MENACHEM BEGIN
> 1977

Prime Minister Menachem Begin of Israel addresses a meeting of prominent Jewish leaders in New York, March 1979. Many Jews worldwide were surprised Begin agreed to take part in peace talks with Egypt.

Egyptian president Anwar Sadat, U.S. president Jimmy Carter, and Begin (from left) listen to their national anthems before the historic meeting in March 1979 to conclude peace negotiations between Egypt and Israel. Carter, who was responsible for arranging the final summit, signed the document as a witness.

half years earlier. Representing Israel was a bespectacled, slightly stocky Prime Minister Menachem Begin, one of the most hawkish and hard-line leaders in Israel's history. Common wisdom had it that one could not find two more unlikely people to agree on terms for peace. Yet there they were, about to sign an agreement that would in many ways change the Middle East forever and send shock waves reverberating throughout the world. If these two men, and these two countries, could make peace, they seemed to be telling the world, then anything was possible. If ever there was a turning point in history, this was it.

To most commentators, Menachem Begin's participation was the more remarkable. His outlook on life had been forged by the Holocaust — the extermination by the Germans of 6 million Jews during World War II. Begin survived the war but lost most of his family, including his mother, in the death camps established by the German Nazis, who controlled the country from 1933 to 1945 under Adolf Hitler. The massive slaughter was part of their plan, known as the "final solution," to rid the world of Jews. Begin was said to feel that, for the Jews, things had not changed very much since then. As he saw it, the Arabs were the latest in a long line of peoples who wanted to persecute and destroy the Jews. Certainly he had some persuasive arguments on his side. In the three decades since Israel's founding in 1948, Arab countries had launched several wars aimed at the destruction of Israel. Although Israel prevailed in all those conflicts, the continual warfare confirmed Begin's view that Arabs were not to be trusted. It was thought that peace was not possible with Begin as head of Israel.

But to the great surprise of nearly everyone, Begin responded quite positively in November 1977 when Sadat, breaking completely with the Arab policy of not recognizing Israel's existence, suggested that the two nations could live side by side in peace. Sadat then made an historic visit to Israel's capital, Jerusalem, a holy city to three of the world's major

An international audience estimated at 100 million watched as the three principals in the Egypt-Israel treaty engaged in a joyous three-way handshake after signing the agreement. It was an especially gratifying moment for Begin, who gave his signature to the first peace treaty in modern Israel's history.

The 7th-century mosque, or Muslim house of worship, called the Dome of the Rock dominates this view of Jerusalem, capital of Israel. Jerusalem is a sacred city to three of the world's major religions: Judaism, Islam, and Christianity.

religions: Judaism, Christianity, and Islam (the religion of Muslims, who believe in Allah as the single deity and in Muhammad as his prophet). It was the first public visit by an Arab leader to Israel. (Sadat's actions did not, at this point, constitute official recognition of Israel but were a significant step in that direction.) Sadat was welcomed heartily in Israel, where he addressed the Israeli parliament, or Knesset, and prayed at Jerusalem's el-Aksa Mosque, the third most sacred shrine of Islam. The visit led to negotiations the following September that were overseen by President Carter and held at Camp David, the woodsy presidential retreat in Maryland. Intense talks over 13 exhausting days and nights produced the framework for an Israeli-Egyptian peace accord that was to lead to an overall Middle East peace settlement, and the two leaders promised to conclude a treaty within months. Both sides subsequently hardened their positions, however, and the joy surrounding the peace talks turned sour. In early March 1979 Begin reported the talks to be "in a state of deep crisis." Finally, a last round of "shuttle diplomacy" by Carter, during which he traveled frequently between Jerusalem and Cairo, the Egyptian capital, to confer with each leader, succeeded in closing the differences between the two sides, setting the stage for the signing of the peace treaty later in the month.

On that festive but tense day in Washington, Begin set aside his distrust and displayed himself as a man of vision. Speaking to the excited onlookers, he quoted the famous words of the prophet Isaiah: "And they shall beat their swords into plowshares,/ And their spears into pruning hooks;/Nation shall not lift up sword against nation,/Neither shall they learn war anymore." He went on to say, "Despite the tragedies and disappointments of the past, we must never forsake that vision, that human dream, that unshakable faith."

Coincidentally, Carter and Sadat used the very same Old Testament words in their speeches. Sadat's remarks included an eloquent pronouncement of his own: "Let there be no more war or bloodshed between Arabs and the Israelis. Let there be no more suffering or denial of rights. Let there be no more despair or loss of faith. Let no mother lament the loss of her child. Let no young man waste his life on a conflict from which no one benefits."

The most dramatic moment of the ceremony occurred after the three leaders had signed the document. (Three copies of the treaty had been prepared — one in English, one in Arabic, and one in Hebrew.) Rising to their feet, the three peacemakers clasped their hands in a three-way handshake and smiled broadly. Carter said to his two guests: "I'm so proud of you." The pact was sealed.

The so-called Camp David treaty, the first peace treaty in Israel's history, was a stunning diplomatic triumph for all three men, but it was also a calculated risk. Neither Carter, Sadat, nor Begin had any illusions that simply signing a piece of paper meant that peace had been achieved. It is said often about the Middle East that peace, like war, has to be waged. Opposition to the treaty was heard even as the three leaders were proclaiming their peaceful intentions. Just yards away, across from the White House in Lafayette Square, angry demonstrators

A poster in Beirut, Lebanon, portrays Sadat as a mixture of Uncle Sam and Moshe Dayan, the Israeli foreign minister. The Arab nations unanimously condemned Sadat as a traitor for opening peace talks with Israel and denounced him as a pawn of the U.S. and Israeli militaries.

chanted "down with the treaty" and "Sadat is a traitor." Throughout the Arab world Sadat was criticized for having made a separate and selfish peace. His fellow Arabs generally held that no agreement with Israel was possible without considering the plight of the Palestinians, who had been displaced from their homes in the land along the eastern shore of the Mediterranean Sea when Israel came into being in 1948. (This was not the only sore point, but it was — and remains — the primary one.) The Camp David treaty mentioned the issue but said too little to please many Arabs other than Egypt's Sadat.

The other Arab countries — such as Syria, Libya, Iraq, Saudi Arabia, Kuwait, and Jordan — were also upset that it was Egypt that decided to seek peace with Israel, for Egypt was not just any Arab country. As the most heavily populated and most heavily armed Arab nation, Egypt was traditionally the Arab

Demonstrators in Beirut protest Sadat's November 1977 visit to Israel, the prelude to the beginning of peace negotiations. Although Sadat's efforts for peace led to the return to Egypt of the Israeli-occupied Sinai Peninsula and elevated his international reputation, his prestige in the Arab world disintegrated.

UPI/BETTMANN NEWSPHOTOS

world's chief representative on the international stage. In the eyes of most Arabs, Egypt was practically committing treason. Palestinians in a refugee camp in Beirut, Lebanon, burned the three leaders in effigy. On the West Bank of the Jordan River — an area captured by Israel from Jordan in the 1967 Arab-Israeli war — widespread demonstrations took place. In Kuwait an angry mob stormed the Egyptian embassy.

Considering the fury of the Arabs, it is ironic that Begin was criticized by some for being too "soft" on the Arabs, for having made too many concessions for the sake of peace, and for not sticking to his own hard-line positions. Among the terms of the agreement was that Israel would return to Egypt the triangular Sinai Peninsula, which lay to the east of Egypt, between that country and Israel. The young nation had captured this region in the 1967 Arab-Israeli war and had since held it as a strategic "buffer zone" against any potential Egyptian attack. Without it, many felt, Israel would be far more vulnerable. But Begin saw that the moment was right to grasp the "olive branch" of peace that had been extended to him. As he said in his speech, "I have signed the treaty of peace with our great neighbor, with Egypt. The heart is full and overflowing." Such are the seeming contradictions that often mark the careers of statesmen, but those judging the life of Menachem Begin would conclude that the contradictions have been few. He had dedicated himself consistently to one thing and one thing only — the welfare and well-being of the Jews and the state of Israel. His actions on March 26, 1979, were in perfect step with this theme.

> *Let us say to one another, and let it be a silent oath between both peoples, Egypt and Israel: no more wars, no more bloodshed, no more threats.*
> —MENACHEM BEGIN

2

The Making of a Rebel

Menachem Begin was born on August 16, 1913, in an Eastern European border town called Brest-Litovsk, the third and last child of Ze'ev Dov and Hassia Begin, who were observant but not strictly Orthodox Jews. His name translates from the Hebrew as "one who consoles," and surely the predicament of his fellow Jews in Europe at the time called for consolation.

In his book about Begin, the well-known Israeli commentator Eitan Haber writes of two striking aspects of a ceremonial gathering for the baby eight days after his birth. First, the infant's godfather was the chief rabbi of Brest-Litovsk; second, the Zionist leadership of the community presented the family with a huge cake shaped like a bouquet of flowers. Both the Orthodox Judaism of the rabbi and the new nationalism symbolized by the cake were formative influences on the young Menachem.

Brest-Litovsk lay at the heart of what was known as the Pale of Settlement, a region along the western frontier of what was then called Russia. (Historically, the word *Russia* refers to the Russian state before the Bolshevik revolution of 1917, which ousted the tsarist autocracy. The country was renamed the Union of Soviet Socialist Republics, or U.S.S.R., and is often referred to as the Soviet Union.) The region was the only place where Jews

> *When we were attacked we would defend ourselves. We never consented to bow down and flee. We would return home bloody and beaten, but always with the awareness that we had not been humiliated.*
> —MENACHEM BEGIN
> on the harassment of Jews in Brest-Litovsk by Polish students

Ze'ev Dov Begin had a great influence on his son Menachem. A scholar and linguist and the local Zionist leader in Brest-Litovsk, Ze'ev Dov instilled in Menachem a deep love of his religion and heritage, the Zionist passion for a Jewish homeland, and an abiding belief in adhering to one's inner convictions in the face of adversity.

PICTURE PEOPLE

The rampant murder and destruction of the pogrom are illustrated in Alton S. Tobey's *The Great Pogrom*. In these wholesale massacres, common throughout eastern Europe and Russia during Begin's childhood, the Jews were made scapegoats for the ills of societies in which anti-Semitism was deeply rooted.

could legally reside. About 5 million Jews lived in the Pale. (The borders of Russia and its neighbors changed frequently over the years as a result of various wars or shifting political alliances. For example, Brest-Litovsk was Russian at the time of Begin's birth, was captured by Germany during World War I, and was incorporated into Poland in 1921. Today it is part of the Soviet Union, which captured the town during World War II.) Within the Pale the Jews lived in poverty and under the constant threat of persecution and periodic massacres known as pogroms. Anti-Semitism, the systematic oppression of Jews as a religious or racial group, became common throughout much of Europe in the late 19th century. Many non-Jews resented the social and economic status of the Jews, and the doctrinal differences between Judaism and Christianity made Jews the targets of superstition and prejudice.

Hostility toward Jews was nothing new. Their entire history, dating back thousands of years, is rife with episodes of violence against them. The most memorable examples from ancient times were the destruction of two glorious temples in Jerusalem. The first was built by King Solomon in the 10th century B.C. It became the center of Jewish religious worship and the symbol of an empire that stretched throughout ancient Palestine, which encompassed today's Israel and parts of Lebanon, Syria, Jordan, and Egypt. The temple was razed by the Babylonians in 586 B.C.; most of the Jews were taken to Babylonia to serve as slaves, an event referred to by the Jews as the Diaspora. In A.D. 66–70 the Romans destroyed a second temple built during a brief resurgence of Jewish power. Once again the Jews were driven into exile. Always, they pledged to return one day.

Anti-Semitism was prevalent in Europe throughout the Middle Ages (roughly, the period from the late 5th through the late 15th centuries). In Christian Europe Jews were scorned and persecuted in the belief that they were responsible for the crucifixion of Jesus Christ. The Crusades, a series of Christian military expeditions that sought to "liberate" the Holy Land from the Muslim "infidels" who

Theodor Herzl was profoundly affected by the Dreyfus case, which he covered for a Viennese newspaper. The Hungarian-born journalist became the leading advocate for the establishment of a separate homeland for the Jews, thus launching the modern Zionist movement.

ruled the region, led to a wave of massacres against the Jews. The first Crusade was launched in the late 11th century; the military marches were held periodically over the next several hundred years. Historians have said the massacres occurred in part because of the heightened religious passions at the time. The Spanish Inquisition — an intensely violent campaign against suspected religious "heretics" that was established in 1478 by King Ferdinand and Queen Isabella of Spain — also prompted the slaughter of Jews. The race was hated also because many Jews had become financiers who were highly influential with the Spanish royal court; thus they were an easy target of the wrath of people oppressed by taxes or other economic hardships. Anti-Semitism plagued Germany, Poland, and Russia throughout the ensuing centuries for many of the same reasons.

One episode of anti-Semitism in France rocked the country and sounded an alarm for the Jews. In the mid-1890s a Jewish army officer named Alfred Dreyfus was convicted of treason for passing important military information to the Germans; he was condemned to life imprisonment on Devil's Island in French Guiana. It was not until 1906 that a court set aside the Dreyfus decision as "wrongful" and "erroneous," but by then the damage had been done. The depth of anti-Semitism in France had been exposed. The Jews were shocked because most of them had thought that France was among the more enlightened and liberal countries in Europe. If such a thing could happen to us here, they thought, we are not safe anywhere.

Among the many people who reached this conclusion was Theodor Herzl, the Paris correspondent of the *Vienna Neue Freie Presse* (Vienna New Free Press). While Herzl was covering the Dreyfus Affair for the paper, he saw mobs shouting "Death to the Jews." He realized then that the only way the Jews could ever hope to live in freedom and with dignity would be if they had a land of their own. He subsequently published a plan for immediate action aimed at establishing a permanent Jewish state in the Jews' ancient homeland of Palestine, then only sparsely populated with Arabs. The idea was not new, but Herzl's tireless work on behalf of it was. He captured the imagination of more and more Jews across Europe. More important, he caught the attention of the statesmen, rulers, and financiers who had the power to determine the fate of Europe and the Near East. To the Jews living in the Pale of Settlement, Herzl's concept of Zionism became the dream that brightened their grim circumstances. (Zion is part of Jerusalem; it is the name given in the Old Testament of the Bible to the city of the Jewish King David and is symbolic of the Jewish desire to establish their homeland in the Holy Land.)

Given the sad history of the Jewish people, the actual birthdate of Menachem Begin is significant. According to the Hebrew calendar, Begin was born on the ninth day of the *Av*, the day on which Jews mourn the many calamities that have befallen them over time. The birthdate seems especially symbolic because Begin, it has been said, is one of those individuals who carried the whole of Jewish suffering on his back.

Begin grew up in a poor home, but one that was warmed by family ties and observance of Jewish law. The single most important influence on Begin throughout his youth was his father, Ze'ev Dov. A Biblical scholar, a lover of languages (he spoke German, Hebrew, Yiddish, Russian, and Polish), and a Zionist, Begin's father believed in Theodor Herzl's call for a Jewish homeland in Palestine. Menachem and Ze'ev Dov went to synagogue every Friday night, and Begin would remain deeply pious and observant of all the commandments of his religion.

Ze'ev Dov made a modest living in the timber trade, but it was as an active member of Brest-Litovsk's many Jewish groups and as a spokesman for the town's Jewish community that he was best known and found his greatest satisfaction.

One day, while Ze'ev was walking with young Menachem and a rabbi, a Polish soldier began harassing them. Suddenly the brutish fellow pulled out a knife, intending to cut off the rabbi's beard — a popular "sport" among anti-Semites. In an attempt to ward off the attack the elder Begin hit the soldier with his cane — an outrageous, defiant act consid-

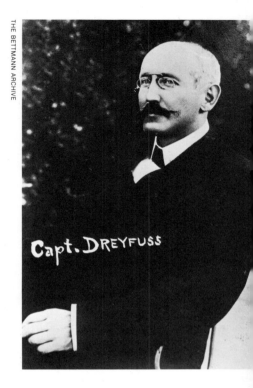

Captain Alfred Dreyfus, a Jewish officer in the French army, became the victim of anti-Semitic persecution when he was wrongfully convicted of treason in 1894. The affair horrified many Jews who considered France a relatively progressive nation.

ering the prevailing climate of hatred against Jews. Ze'ev Dov and the rabbi were arrested and whipped but were eventually released. As Menachem Begin recalled the incident in a 1970s interview: "My father returned home badly beaten, but he was in good spirits, for he was convinced he had done what was right, though it might have cost him his life. We were all very proud of our father's behavior — an example for all of the inhabitants of the Jewish community. Incidentally, he subsequently received a letter of apology from the military authorities."

On another occasion, Ze'ev Dov was bold enough to speak out against Jozef Pilsudski, the Polish leader and national hero who had played a large role

As a high-school student in the then Polish city of Brest-Litovsk, Begin avidly read works on Jewish history and culture. He studied Herzl's Zionist manifesto *Der Judenstaat* (The Jewish State), absorbing ideas that would direct the course of his life.

DER

JUDENSTAAT.

VERSUCH

EINER

MODERNEN LÖSUNG DER JUDENFRAGE

VON

THEODOR HERZL

DOCTOR DER RECHTE.

LEIPZIG und WIEN 1896.

M. BREITENSTEIN'S VERLAGS-BUCHHANDLUNG

WIEN, IX., WÄHRINGERSTRASSE 5.

in the establishment of the Polish nation after World War I. Pilsudski had come to Brest-Litovsk to look into charges that the Jews — again the scapegoats — were running an extensive black market, trading illegally in various goods. He demanded that the Jews begin informing on other Jews who were supposedly creating shortages of vital goods so that their illicit trade would flourish. Ze'ev enraged Pilsudski by replying, to his face, that "We are not detectives, nor are we informers. The Jewish community has no secret police. The authorities, however, do have a secret police. Let them do the job."

Such bravery was risky for a member of an oppressed community. Indeed, some people feared that such comments would trigger more pogroms. This very debate — between those Jews who prefer to simply accept a bad situation in hopes that the trouble will soon disappear and those who want to fight on behalf of their dignity — has been an ongoing one for Jews. Begin himself believed in the "stand and fight" ethic from the first. As he once said, "This world does not pity the slaughtered. It only respects those who fight."

Menachem Begin entered the Mizrachi (Orthodox) elementary school in Brest-Litovsk at the age of seven. When he made his first public speech at the

German soldiers watch as Brest-Litovsk burns in 1915. After World War I many peoples in eastern and central Europe, under the principle of self-determination, established their own nations. This prevailing mood of nationalism sharpened the Zionists' urge for a Jewish nation in Palestine.

tender age of 12, his talent for powerful oratory was obvious. He spoke at a ceremony celebrating Lag B'Omer, the Jewish feast dedicated to young students (holidays were the few occasions on which the Jewish community could temporarily forget its woes), addressing hundreds of Jews from atop a table. His sister, Rachel, later remembered that "he held them spellbound."

At the age of 13 Begin had his bar mitzvah — the rite of initiation into the full responsibilities of the Jewish faith. Begin then entered the Polish gymnasium, or high school, where he excelled in the humanities.

His pride and stubborn will were evident from the very start. Only three Jews were in the school, but Begin was not in the least fazed by being in such a minority. When an important Latin exam was scheduled for Saturday, the Jewish Sabbath, Begin told his teacher that he was forbidden by Jewish law to write on that day. The other children laughed at him; the teacher gave him a failing mark.

According to Eitan Haber, Begin said later: "I might have given in and written the exam, but they

Young Jewish students in postwar Vilna, capital of Lithuania, arrive at school. Begin gave early evidence of both his gift for oratory — he made his first speech at the age of 12 — and his strong leadership qualities — he taught his fellow Jewish schoolmates to stand up to their persecutors.

laughed, and I wasn't going to let them think that I surrendered because of their laughter."

Begin immersed himself in Jewish studies. Among the books that most greatly interested him were the Bible; Herzl's *Der Judenstaat* (The Jewish State); *Rome and Jerusalem* by Moses Hess, an ardent believer in the religious need for a homeland in Palestine; and *Autoemancipation*, by Leon Pinsker, a Zionist leader and theorist who argued that anti-Semitism was inevitable in Gentile (non-Jewish) societies and that the solution was for the Jews to form a nation on land of their own.

All these books served as inspiration for Begin's emerging Zionist sensibilities. Of equal importance was what he experienced in the streets. As he once said, "I remember two things from my childhood: Jews being persecuted and the courage of the Jew. . . . We were persecuted by the anti-Semites, even at public school, and we had to defend ourselves, and we did."

Though he was neither tall nor very muscular, Menachem Begin always refused to submit to the anti-Semitic attacks to which he was subjected, and his aggressive stance made him a leader at the gymnasium and later at the University of Warsaw, where he enrolled as a law student in 1931. Begin recounted later that he and his friends would defend themselves whenever they were attacked and would never submit or run away. Thus, even though they returned home "bloody and beaten" on occasion, they never felt that they had been humiliated.

His increasing militancy, coupled with his impressive intellectual and linguistic skills, made Begin a prime candidate to become an activist for Jewish rights and a campaigner for a Jewish homeland. At 15 he began to fulfill that potential by joining *Betar*, a Zionist youth movement that set him on the path he would follow for the rest of his life.

> *We are a people—one people. We are strong enough to form a state and indeed a model state.*
> —THEODOR HERZL
> in *The Jewish State*

3

From the Ghetto to the Gulag

I was fascinated by the total Zionism of Betar," Menachem Begin once recalled. "I had no doubt whatsoever that this was the movement in which I would want to serve the Jewish people all my life." More than Betar itself, though, it was the group's leader — Vladimir Ze'ev Jabotinsky — who inspired the young Begin to such passionate devotion. Said Begin years later: "My entire life has been influenced by him, both in the underground and in politics; the willingness to fight for the liberation of the homeland, and the logical analysis of facts in political matters." Begin revered Jabotinsky; in order to understand Begin, one must first understand Jabotinsky and his ideals.

Vladimir Ze'ev Jabotinsky was born in 1880 in Odessa, a Russian port city on the Black Sea. He worked as a foreign correspondent in Switzerland and in Italy, where he also studied law and Italian history. It wasn't until just after the turn of the century that he became part of the Zionist movement. As his ideas evolved over the next few decades, they revealed a man of militant — some said violent — outlook, who stressed the importance of self-defense and the willingness to fight for one's rights. Jabotinsky believed that given the reality of global politics — that power and force often carried the day — Zionists should receive military training and be

> *Jabotinsky to us was more than a leader, he was the bearer of hope. We looked to him to bring us out of bondage. He would bring about the setting up of the state of Israel.*
> —MENACHEM BEGIN
> on Vladimir Jabotinsky

Begin poses with his new bride, Aliza Arnold, in May 1939, on the eve of the Nazi invasion of Poland. Both committed to the goal of a Jewish state in Palestine, Menachem and Aliza worked as Zionist activists in Warsaw before their world crumbled with the coming of World War II. The war would separate the couple for two years.

PICTURE PEOPLE

Vladimir Jabotinsky was the Russian originator of Revisionist Zionism, a radical minority position within the Zionist movement. In the face of the Nazi threat, Jabotinsky was convinced that the establishment of a Jewish homeland in Palestine was necessary for the very survival of the Jewish people.

prepared to defend their homeland. As history had taught the Jews that they could not rely on others to protect them, the time had come to protect themselves. According to Israeli journalist Amos Elon, "Jabotinsky preached the conquest of Palestine through the sword."

Founded in 1925, his Revisionist party believed in putting firm and consistent pressure on Great Britain, which had been given a mandate to administer Palestine during the peace negotiations after World War I, to grant the Jews a homeland there. Jabotinsky believed that Britain had committed itself to a Jewish homeland by virtue of the Balfour Declaration, issued by British foreign minister Arthur Balfour in 1917. The Balfour Declaration pledged British support for the establishment of a Jewish state in Palestine. The British were gentlemen, said Jabotinsky; if pressured strongly, even opposed, they would live up to the Balfour Declaration.

Other Zionist leaders disagreed. Great Britain controlled a vast colonial empire and in the years before World War II was the most powerful nation in the world. The decision of its leaders regarding Palestine would be based on a number of geopolitical considerations, not the least of which was the self-interest of the British empire. Chaim Weizmann, one of the leading Zionists of the day, believed that the Jewish nation could best be achieved through diplomacy and quiet, behind-the-scenes lobbying; the Balfour Declaration had been achieved in such fashion. The British were not likely to respond well to direct pressure.

The Labor Zionism of David Ben-Gurion came to the forefront of the Zionist movement in the early 1930s. Ben-Gurion believed that Jews should immigrate to Palestine, settle and work the land there, and establish national institutions in preparation for the day of Jewish independence.

Some historians have speculated that it was Jabotinsky's admiration for Italy, and in particular for Giuseppe Garibaldi and other Italian soldier/nationalists who played crucial roles in the formation of modern Italy, that bred in him a belief in the power of force. Whatever the case, his brand of "muscular

YIVO INSTITUTE FOR JEWISH RESEARCH

Zionism" greatly appealed to Begin. When the youth arrived in the Polish capital of Warsaw to begin law studies there, he reported without delay to the offices of the *Betar* high commission. (Founded in 1923, Betar was a Zionist youth group dedicated to implementing the ideals of Jabotinsky.)

Begin quickly became one of Betar's leading speakers and activists in Poland and was subsequently sent to Czechoslovakia to continue his work. As one leading Betar figure recalled: "I know that for months on end Begin made do with only one meal a day, and I received reports . . . that he was seen in Prague sleeping on a bench in one of the city's public parks. Begin never thought about himself and never complained. As far as he was concerned, the main thing was to carry out his mission. That was the operative word with Begin — a sense of 'mission.' " As the 1930s wore on, it became clear that Begin had become Jabotinsky's heir apparent.

The Revisionists were constantly criticized by their fellow Zionists. David Ben-Gurion, who later would become prime minister of Israel, and others were appalled by the fact that Betar members wore uniforms and were trained in the use of weapons, not unlike the fascist youth movements of the time, most notably those sponsored by the virulently anti-Semitic Nazi party in Germany. The Labor Zionists also recoiled from such typical Jabotinsky pronouncements as, "If you don't know how to shoot, you have no hope. But if you know how to shoot, you have some hope." Ben-Gurion even went

Members of a *Betar* group in Poland gather in the early 1930s for a portrait. Betar members learned essential military training and survival techniques with the understanding that they might have to fight for Palestine.

so far as to compare the Betar leader with Adolf Hitler, the German Nazi leader, and Benito Mussolini, the Italian Fascist dictator. The 1933 assassination in Tel Aviv of Chaim Arlosoroff, a leading Labor Zionist, by men reportedly connected with the Revisionists brought the group even more criticism. After the killing, Begin's mother was asked, "Your son's a good boy, but why does he mix with those murderers?"

Although the Revisionists were ostracized, their numbers increased, to some 70,000 in 700 branches in Poland. At the same time, attacks against Jewish students — at the gymnasium in Brest-Litovsk and at the University of Warsaw — diminished under the threat of Jewish retaliation. Begin was convinced that Jabotinsky's principles worked.

In April 1939 Jabotinsky appointed Begin the Betar commissioner for Poland. Begin celebrated the promotion by staging a demonstration outside the British embassy in Warsaw to protest that country's strictures against Jewish immigration to Palestine. Begin had grown increasingly militant. The previous year at a worldwide Betar conference, he had quarrelled with Jabotinsky over Begin's advocacy of open, armed rebellion against the British in Palestine. Jabotinsky sharply disagreed; opposition was one thing, revolt another. After the Warsaw demonstration Begin was arrested and held for three weeks, during which time his head was shaved. It

A Warsaw street scene from the 1920s. Begin, who arrived in the Polish capital in 1931 to study law, quickly joined the local Betar organization in order to continue his Zionist activities. By 1939 the Betar group in Poland numbered some 70,000 members, and Begin was appointed its commissioner.

was to be the first of many encounters with police and prison.

That same spring also brought enormous joy to Menachem Begin's life. Because he had no money for hotels or restaurants, he stayed in the homes of leaders of the Revisionist party and of fellow Betar members while he worked for the Zionist organization. It was in the home of Zvi Arnold, relative of a Revisionist party member, that Begin met his host's twin daughters, Leah and Aliza.

The small, vivacious pair were in their late teens and actively involved in Betar. Begin recalled that when he first saw the sisters: "I looked at one of them and said to myself, 'That one is going to be my wife,' although I was much older. I was an old man of twenty-six!"

The young woman who had caught Begin's eye was Aliza. They were married a month later in the synagogue of the small Polish town of Drohobycz. According to Begin biographer Eric Silver, Aliza wore "a well-cut knee length coat and rakish hat, the lean, bespectacled Menachem [was dressed] in a pale, shapeless mackintosh. . . . Jabotinsky came by train from Paris for the wedding."

The marriage was to last until the death of Ala (as Begin always called her) 43 years later, surviving the stresses of war, exile, separation, and politics. Although Aliza was as committed to the Jewish

Nazi storm troopers parade at a rally in Nuremberg in the mid-1930s. Hitler's grand show of force preceded the promulgation of the 1935 Nuremberg Laws, which stripped German Jews of their rights as citizens, beginning their long nightmare under the Nazi regime.

homeland as her husband was, she was content to remain behind the scenes. Her twin Leah, like most of Begin's family, would die in the Holocaust during World War II.

The couple had no honeymoon. Begin left the day after the wedding for Warsaw, where he organized the transport of Jewish immigrants to Palestine. As events in Europe brought war closer, immigration and the establishment of the Jewish state became even more crucial for Zionists. The British, through the White Paper of 1939 (a "white paper" is a government report), had severely restricted Jewish immigration to Palestine. With the rise to power of Adolf Hitler and the launching of the Holocaust, intended to eradicate Europe's Jews, the freedom to immigrate to Palestine and the establishment of the Jewish homeland was no longer merely a political matter. For the Jews, it meant survival.

Hitler came to power by portraying himself as a powerful leader devoted to the German "fatherland." The image appealed to many Germans in part because of their country's devastating loss in World War I and because of crushing economic difficulties at home. Hitler also advanced racial policies declaring the Germans to be a "pure" race destined to rule the world. The Jews, he claimed, had "soiled" the Germans, were responsible for all of society's ills, and needed to be destroyed. Jews in Germany faced constant harassment and humiliation. They were discriminated against in terms of jobs, housing, and education and were beaten, boycotted, and forced to live in ghettos. Such appalling practices became official through the Nuremberg Laws of 1935. On the night of November 7, 1938, Hitler's storm troopers destroyed and burned homes, synagogues, and shops owned by Jews, and beat and arrested vast numbers of people. Known as *Kristallnacht* (Crystal Night) because of the multitude of shattered glass, it marked the beginning of Hitler's "final solution" to the "Jewish problem." Jews were shipped to death camps; most were killed outright, others were used as slaves and then were murdered. In the next few years, millions of Jews died in the camps. Their bodies were cremated — after the Nazis had taken their jewelry, gold teeth, hair, and clothes.

As Hitler consolidated his dictatorial powers within Germany, he took aggressive military actions aimed at dominating Europe. In 1938 Germany occupied Austria and parts of Czechoslovakia. In 1939 Germany swallowed the rest of that country, forged a military alliance with Italy (which had, under the dictatorship of Benito Mussolini, invaded Albania), and began to threaten Poland. In late August 1939 Germany and the Soviet Union signed a nonaggression pact pledging that neither would attack the other. The agreement shocked Europe. Hitler had declared his fascist doctrine of National Socialism (from whence the term "Nazi" is derived) to be unalterably opposed to communism. As the leader of the world's only communist state, Joseph Stalin was similarly ill-disposed toward Nazism. More important, the nonaggresson pact removed the last obstacle — the huge Soviet military — to Nazi aggression. France and Great Britain, while opposed to the German actions, had been slow to realize the danger posed by Nazism and were not yet prepared to fight.

On September 1, as expected, Hitler's armies invaded Poland with a lightning-quick tank and plane attack that easily overcame the Polish forces, some of whom were fighting on horseback. Two days later France and Great Britain declared war on Germany.

A pre-World War II postcard depicts Jews emigrating from Europe. As the Nazis increased their hold over Germany, Jews throughout Europe left their homes. Thousands entered Palestine illegally, swelling the Jewish population and alarming the colonial British government there.

As the Nazi bombs rained down on Warsaw, Menachem and Aliza Begin were in the city weighing their next move. Begin, foreseeing the inevitability of the Nazi onslaught, had spent most of his time in the previous months helping Jews flee Poland; the plan was for them eventually to arrive in Palestine through a network that passed through Romania and used ports on the Black Sea. Now, because of the war, these trips had become virtually impossible. The Begins, commiserating in the Betar headquarters in Warsaw, were approached by a fellow member. "Why are you still here?" he asked Begin. "We've got passports for you and Aliza for Palestine. Take them and go!" But Begin decided not to leave, saying that "flight is the road of despair." The Nazi *Blitzkrieg* — the word means "lightning war" — had enraged him not only as a Jew but as a loyal Pole, and he wanted to help defend the country, even at great personal risk.

Friends prevailed upon him to at least leave Warsaw, and so he and Aliza made their way northeast, to Vilna, in neighboring Lithuania. Vilna had long been a center of Jewish learning and culture; now it would also serve as a base for Betar to help Jews escape from the Nazis. Hundreds of Jewish refugees flowed into the city. All the while Begin was convinced that the Polish, with the help of the British and French, would eventually turn back the Germans. At the same time, however, the Soviets were advancing on Vilna, having been freed by the nonaggression pact to pursue their own expansionist designs. They were no friends of the Zionists either.

In the summer of 1940 Britain was still not ready to fight; there would be no rescue for Poland. France fell to the Germans. The Soviets entered Vilna, poised to take control. Betar members were further disheartened by the news that Jabotinsky had died while in the United States. In September the Soviet secret police, who had been tailing Begin and monitoring his activities (Zionist activities were a crime under Soviet law), finally caught up with him. He had ignored a summons to appear at the Vilna town hall, a summons he knew was really a ploy designed to capture him. Begin refused to go into hiding, however, saying, "If the Soviet Government . . . wants to arrest me, let its agents put themselves out and come to my house. That is their job. Why should I disappear as if the earth had swallowed me up?"

Begin had another reason for his willingness to be arrested. It had to do with his mentor's death. As he said, "After the death of Jabotinsky, the whole world blackened for me. . . I was ready to be arrested by the Soviets because, as I said at the grave of a member of the Betar, 'If we can't fight for our country, then we shall suffer for it.' "

Finally, three Lithuanian intelligence agents arrived at the Begin apartment, showing up in the middle of a chess game between Begin and Yisrael Sheib, who with his wife shared the flat with Begin and Aliza. Sheib recalled the arrest as follows:

"Menachem was most polite to his guests. He asked them to come in and make themselves comfortable while he dressed. He even invited them to have tea, but they declined. Then Menachem polished his shoes, put on his best suit, carefully knotted his necktie, and asked permission to take along some books. 'No need,' one of the men said. 'You'll be back before long.' But Begin refused to go without at least his Bible, which he took down from its accustomed place and tucked under his arm. At the door, he stopped, turned, and said, 'After you, gentlemen. This is my house, and I would not dream of allowing my guests to leave after me.' He embraced me and my wife, Batya, who burst into tears. But young Aliza — she was only twenty at the time — retained her composure. She was allowed to accompany her husband to the car parked outside, and there they said their goodbyes. Before they parted, Menachem told Aliza to tell me that he conceded the chess game because I was ahead when we were interrupted."

> *I am certain that if I filled whole pages I could not even attempt to explain what the death of the head of Betar meant to me. . . . I felt the bearer of hope was gone.*
> —MENACHEM BEGIN
> on the death of
> Vladimir Jabotinsky

4

White Nights

The Soviet intelligence officer addressed the captive in Vilna's Lukishki prison.

"I tell you, you are a big, political criminal. You are worse than a man who has murdered ten people."

"But why? Why?" responded Menachem Begin, determined to maintain his honor.

"Because all your activities were anti-Soviet and anti-revolutionary. . . Jabotinsky was the leader of Jewish fascism."

"I am a prisoner and I know I have to answer questions," replied the captive. "But I will defend the honor of my teacher as long as I am able to do so. Wouldn't you . . . do the same thing if someone were to offend the memory of Lenin?"

With such responses, Menachem Begin engaged in a spirited, intellectual debate with his captors and proved himself to be their superior. One historian has said that Begin was able to hold out by viewing his incarceration and his relationship with the Soviet interrogators as a "deadly game of chess." Most other prisoners, it seemed, lacked Begin's fortitude. In Begin's case strength meant strength of the mind, not of the body, for Begin, slim and bespectacled, appeared on the outside to be physically frail and meek. Yet men more robust than he withered under the prison experience. Some died, while others confessed to crimes they did not commit. Begin would do neither.

He was sentenced to eight years in prison as "an

History tells us of underground movements that were formed by citizens against their powerful rulers; but in the Soviet Union the rulers have created a powerful underground against their citizens.
—MENACHEM BEGIN
on the Soviet police

Begin, shown here in a Betar uniform, was arrested in Vilna in September 1940 for his Zionist activities, which were illegal under the communist Soviet regime.

element dangerous to society" and spent the first nine months of the sentence in Lukishki prison. There he was subjected to endless questioning and taunting, placed in solitary confinement, deprived of sleep, and forced to subsist on a diet of thin porridge. Begin's extraordinary willpower was constantly in evidence. On Yom Kippur, the Day of Atonement and the most holy of all days for Jews, Begin staunchly fasted, in accordance with Jewish law. Despite the fact that he had been poorly nourished for nearly a year, Begin was stoic enough to donate his meager rations to his cellmates. On another occasion, the Soviet agents, trying to get him to "tell the truth," forced him to sit for 60 hours in a chair with his knees pressed against a wall and his eyes focused on one spot. Only by remaining silent and conjuring up the brighter moments of his past was he able to endure such psychological torture.

Solitary confinement was another variation on the nearly intolerable. After a prison guard overheard Begin telling a joke to fellow prisoners about a nitwit and thought Begin was discussing him personally, the prison superintendent to whom the incident was reported ordered Begin thrown into solitary. For seven days he was confined without blanket or pail to a black, windowless cell that during the day was excruciatingly hot and airless and at night was bitterly cold. Any attempt to sleep involved lying on the cement floor, fending off rats.

Begin found sustenance in the Bible, in limited contacts with the small group of fellow Jewish activists also imprisoned at Lukishki, and with the hope that Aliza had made her way safely to Palestine. His stubborn character also served him well. Silver says that when Begin finally did confess, he did so entirely on his own terms. The Soviet interrogators wanted him to sign a statement that read, "I admit I am guilty of having been the chairman of the Betar organization in Poland." After hours and hours of argument that lasted through the night, Begin somehow managed to persuade his interrogator to delete the reference to guilt, so that the confession was merely factual: "I admit that I was chairman of the Betar of Poland." Silver says that "the interrogator, like others with whom Begin was to negotiate, was worn down by attrition. 'I never want to see you again,' he [the Soviet official] yelled as his tormentor was led back to his cell."

In May 1941, 2,000 Lukishki prisoners were told they were being transferred and that they would be allowed to have a farewell visit by one relative. Begin, thinking that his wife might still be in Vilna, hoping for his release, asked to see her. Instead, Paula Daiches, a woman slightly resembling Aliza, appeared and told him, "Aunt Ala is with Uncle Shimshon." Begin understood. Ala was Aliza's nickname, and Shimshon was Shimshon Juniczman, the Betar leader in Palestine. Daiches went on to say that "your brothers" — which Begin took to mean his Betar comrades — "are also well. They are also with Aunt Ala."

The glad tidings were short-lived. The following month, Begin and the others were forced to undertake a 6-week, 1,500-mile journey to the Pechor-Lag work camp, near the icy Barents Sea just south of the Arctic Circle. The trip was a nightmare. Seventy passengers were jammed into railroad cars intended to accommodate 40 people or 8 horses. A single pipe opening functioned as the only lavatory. Two tiny hatches provided "ventilation." Salted fish and bread were the only food, and water, sometimes taken from muddy trackside puddles alive with frogs, was passed around in a communal bucket. Begin later wrote: "The train rocked us about like a ship pitching and tossing in a stormy sea. Many of us became train-sick and vomited continuously. Our strength was exhausted. We dozed. No one spoke any longer."

Work camps such as Pechor-Lag — the entire Soviet penal system was known as the gulag — were established in the 1930s at the behest of Soviet leader Joseph Stalin as part of his efforts to purge Soviet society of reactionary elements. The country had undergone a revolution in 1917 in which the Communists, or Bolsheviks, had come to power. Two decades later the country still desperately needed modernization and industrialization. Any "counterrevolutionary" activities, such as resisting changes in agricultural policies or speaking out

From a poster attached to an apartment complex, a benevolent-looking Joseph Stalin watches Leningrad pedestrians in 1936. Underneath the glowing official reports of Soviet life lay the grim realities of the Stalinist labor camps.

Stalin speaks with his foreign minister, Vyacheslav Molotov, at Yalta in February 1945, two months before the surrender of Germany. Stalin's ambitions for Soviet domination of postwar Eastern Europe meant that returning Jews faced the bitter prospect of living under hostile communist regimes.

against any of the concepts of the revolution, were severely punished, most often by executions and exile to Siberia, the vast, harsh, sparsely populated part of the country east of the Ural Mountains. The prisoners of the gulag were put to work — building railroads and highways, clearing forests, mining. Repression under Stalin of such "enemies of the people" and the associated famines caused by the forced "collectivization" of agriculture (the organization of farms into large units operated under governmental supervision) claimed millions of lives.

Begin arrived at Pechor-Lag to the grim comment of a Soviet soldier. "You'll get used to it," the man said, referring to the routinely sub-zero temperatures and almost intolerable way of life at the work camp. "If you don't, you'll die."

Begin had cause to wonder whether he would survive in this land where winter was nine months long. The hospital where he spent his first week was a mile from the bathhouse, and patients had to run half-naked in the painful cold to reach it. His bed was infested with bugs that kept him awake every night. He was soon put to work building a railway. For 14 hours every day he was forced to carry heavy iron rails, one on each bony shoulder, a quarter of a mile, back and forth, from a ship on the Pechora River to a rail truck. Mosquitoes plagued him throughout. "They sting and sting," lamented Begin, "drink and buzz. There is no escaping them." Life for most gulag prisoners was brutal and short, a daily struggle for survival. Begin wrote later, "On the banks of the Pechora, I found animals walking on two legs."

Despite the hardships, Begin responded to the natural beauty of the camp with an exuberance that is hard to imagine. "The north! Where the sun rises the moment it sets in the summer and the northern dawn lights up the nights in the winter. What a miraculous phenomenon! How stunningly beautiful it is! And how awe-inspiring in its beauty!" he wrote later. Another prisoner captured the paradox of life in Pechor-Lag: "Our days are black, and our nights are white!"

The irony was not lost on Begin. Years later he wrote a memoir of his time in prison. The London

Times called the book, published as *White Nights* in 1957, "one of the greatest pieces of prison literature in the world." It contained this passage: "The German extermination camps and the Russian labor camps were, the one as much as the other, works of the devil. But even the devil's works are various. The difference between the German death camps and the Soviet concentration camps lies in one small word, and a whole world of difference lies in it: hope. The German exterminators gave their victims no prospect of living; the prisoners in the Soviet labor camps have such a chance. In most cases it is a very slight chance, but even a slight prospect is still a chance."

Begin's work gang consisted of Jews, Russians, Poles, Lithuanians, Latvians, Estonians, and Romanians, a motley crew ranging from outright criminals to political prisoners like Begin. They all worked on the railway and were fed according to the amount of work they completed. Jews, as usual, were also subject to anti-Semitic harassment. The cold, the backbreaking labor, and the daily degradation were so extreme that one historian wrote that "a will to survive alone could not have ensured his survival."

One morning a rumor swept the camp: all Polish prisoners were to be freed. Apparently, the Polish

> *Humanity is still waiting for the revolutions of revolutions that will not exchange prisoners but do away with prisons.*
> —MENACHEM BEGIN

AP/WIDE WORLD PHOTOS

Weary German prisoners of war huddle under blankets to ward off the Russian cold, 1942. The Nazi invasion of the Soviet Union in June 1941 proved a blessing for Begin when the Soviets released their Polish prisoners to join the fight against the Germans.

government leaders who had fled when Germany invaded Poland and the Soviet government had agreed that all Polish prisoners were to be released so that they could join in the fight against Germany, which had, despite the nonaggression agreement with the Soviet Union, attacked the Soviets in 1941.

Sure enough, the Stalin-Sikorski agreement, between the Soviet leader and General Wladyslaw Sikorski, prime minister of the Polish government in exile, led to Begin's release. He and the other Poles were supposed to join the Polish army, but Begin's sights were on Palestine. For several months in the latter part of 1941 he was one of many refugees wandering through Soviet Central Asia, sleeping in railway stations and public parks, going hungry most of the time, surviving, somehow, without money. Thoughts of his homeland were enough to keep him going. As he said later, "I could hear the whirring wings of freedom."

By pure chance he was reunited with his sister, Rachel. Dozing on a railway platform while waiting to try and catch a ride south, he overheard someone mention the name Halperin, the name of his sister's husband. As it turned out, the Halperin being spoken of was indeed Rachel's husband, a remarkable coincidence considering the millions of families separated by the war who were destined never to see each other again. Begin's joy at being reunited with his sister soon was overlaid with the sorrow of not knowing the fate of his father, mother, and brother. It was not until 1946 that Begin and Rachel learned that the rest of their family was dead, victims of the Nazis.

Begin stayed for a while with his sister, gradually regaining his strength. Ever fearful of the Soviet authorities, he then decided to step up his efforts to reach Palestine. Obtaining an exit visa was out of the question. Instead, he tried to join the Polish army, which it was said would eventually be sent to the increasingly important Middle East theater of the war. This course of action was considered a real gamble, as there was no guarantee, only a general feeling, that the army would be dispatched to the

Forced by the Allied liberation troops to confront the monstrosities of the Nazi death camps, these German civilians dispose of corpses at Bergen-Belsen, 1945.

Middle East. Still, Begin thought it a risk worth taking.

Begin failed his first army physical. "You are a man with a serious heart ailment," said the doctor. "Your vision is very faulty. You will never be able to shoot properly." Begin subsequently sought help from fellow Betar members, also living in exile in the Soviet Union, who had managed to establish a rapport with some influential people. The next time around, Begin's physical examination had very different results. "Heart and lungs — excellent," pronounced the doctor. "You are actually shortsighted, but in the army you'll learn to shoot properly. If you try, you'll still be one of our best marksmen."

As Frank Gervasi put it in *The Life and Times of Menahem Begin*: "He was undoubtedly the most unsoldierly looking soldier in the entire outfit, thin to the point of scrawniness and wearing thick eyeglasses." A few weeks later, however, he reached his homeland.

5

A New Life in the Holy Land

In May 1942 Menachem Begin was sent with the Polish army to Jerusalem, where the exhausted, emaciated private was soon reunited with Aliza, who was living there. In March 1943, the couple's first child, a son named Binyamin, was born. The young *sabra*, or native-born Israeli, and his father, still a newcomer to the Holy Land, had arrived in a land of unquestionable beauty, unceasing turmoil, and an uncertain future.

The return of the Jews to Palestine had begun in the late 19th century. Spurred by the work of Theodor Herzl and other Zionist thinkers and by difficult living conditions in Europe, Jews left the continent behind to form agricultural settlements in the Holy Land, to move into Jewish quarters in Jerusalem or the port city of Haifa, or to form Jewish towns and villages, most notably the city of Tel Aviv. By 1914 about 60,000 Jews were living in Palestine, along with 70,000 Christians and 500,000 Muslims. The country was ruled at the time by the Ottoman Turks, who had added Palestine to their empire in the early 16th century. The Turks were wary of the increased number of Jews in the country because most were involved in business or com-

> *We did not take strange land; we returned to our homeland. The link between our nation and this land is eternal.*
> —MENACHEM BEGIN

Muslims celebrate a religious holiday in Jerusalem, 1903. As Jewish immigration to Palestine increased during the 1920s and 1930s, the Palestinian Arabs felt threatened by the very real prospect of the creation of a Jewish state on the land they considered their own.

Begin (second from right), in the uniform of a Polish soldier, poses with Aliza and friends in Palestine. Begin arrived in 1942 and was reunited with his wife, who had immigrated after his arrest.

merce with foreign powers, and the Turks feared foreign interference in the administration of their empire. The local Arab population also was alarmed by the prospect of Jewish statehood, worried that the Jews would rob them of their livelihoods and banish them from their land.

World War I, which lasted from 1914 to 1918, led to the dissolution of the Ottoman Empire and dramatic changes for Palestine. British and French forces drove the Turks and Germans out of the country, and Great Britain was later granted the mandate to administer Palestine. In 1917, just before the military victory in Palestine, Arthur Balfour pledged British support for a Jewish homeland in Palestine: "His Majesty's government views with favor the establishment in Palestine of a national home for the Jewish people and will use their best endeavors to facilitate the achievement of that object, it being clearly understood that nothing shall be done which may prejudice the civil and religious rights and political rights of existing non-Jewish communities in Palestine, or the rights and political status enjoyed by Jews in any other country." The statement was seen as a major victory for Chaim Weizmann, who had assumed leadership of the Zionist movement after Herzl's death in 1904, and seemed to legitimize the Jewish quest for a homeland. The language of Zionists, referring to a national home for the Jewish people, had become the language of the world's most powerful government.

Immigration increased. By 1922, 100,000 Jews were in Palestine; by 1935, 250,000. The influx was coordinated by the two main Zionist bodies, the World Zionist Organization and the Jewish Agency. While still a majority, the Arabs realized that this would not be so for long if the rate of Jewish immigration continued unchecked. Arab resistance was very strong, and the two groups often clashed. Arab riots occurred in Jerusalem in 1920, in Jaffa

British soldiers question a local Arab after a riot in which an airport was put to the torch. In the 1917 Balfour Declaration, Britain offered its support for the establishment of a Jewish homeland in Palestine, seemingly ignoring the desires of thousands of Palestinian Arabs already living there.

in 1921, again in Jerusalem in 1929, and an organized rebellion lasted from 1936 through 1939. Despite the inflamed passions, Jews kept streaming into Palestine. The rise of Hitler caused the Jewish presence there to nearly double; by 1939 some 450,000 Jews had entered the country. Having seen the Arab states of Syria, Transjordan, and Iraq move toward independence and autonomy, the Palestinian Arabs called for a state of their own. Britain was caught in the middle, apparently at a loss as to how to reconcile the competing claims. Order was kept primarily through the threat of force.

Fearful that the Arabs might align themselves with Germany to achieve their aims (as they had fought with the British during World War I to throw off the Ottoman Empire), in 1939 Britain issued a white paper that decreed that Jewish immigration to Palestine would end following the admission of 75,000 immigrants over the next five years. The white paper also sought to limit Jewish purchases of Arab land and said that British policy did not back the establishment of a Jewish state in Pales-

Russian chemist Chaim Weizmann took up the reins of Zionist leadership after the death of Herzl in 1904. Weizmann felt that a Jewish state could be founded without bloodshed by negotiating with the British authorities and incorporating the Palestinian Arabs.

tine. The Zionists were outraged. As arguments erupted over the white paper's intent, World War II took center stage.

During the war, both the Jews and Arabs observed a relative truce with the British, who were consumed by the effort, in alliance with the United States, France, and others, to defeat the Axis powers of Germany and Italy. Cooperation with the British put the Zionists in a particularly difficult situation, however. On the one hand, the British were fighting against the Hitler menace, to the obvious benefit of Jews and non-Jews everywhere. Accordingly, more than 30,000 Palestinian Jews joined the Allied armies. Begin was initially swayed by this argument. Unlike the many refugees who deserted the Polish army upon its arrival in Palestine, Begin felt bound to honor his commitment and remained in the army until December 1943. On the other hand, Britain repeatedly refused to ease its immigration policies regarding Palestine, turning a cold shoulder on desperate European Jews for whom escape to Palestine was their last hope. This apparent indifference to the fate of the Jews, coupled with the British repudiation of the Balfour Declaration, further infuriated the Zionists. They reacted by deciding to bring Jews into Palestine illegally.

The British responded by refusing to allow ships carrying illegal Jewish immigrants entry to Palestine. In one instance several ships, carrying thousands of European refugees who had managed to reach Romanian and Turkish ports, were turned away from the shores of Palestine by British authorities. Some of the refugees were sent back where they had come from; others were placed in internment camps on the island of Cyprus, south of Turkey. Some of the would-be immigrants were expelled even after they had set foot on land and kissed the beach out of sheer joy at their arrival. One group of Jews blew up their ship, the S.S. *Patria*, rather than comply with an order by the British high commissioner for Palestine to sail for the island of Mauritius in the Indian Ocean. More than 250 men, women, and children drowned as a result of this act of defiance.

Has not the time come to convert Jewish solidarity from a gentile myth to a Jewish reality?
—MENACHEM BEGIN

> *There are times when everything in you cries out: your very self-respect as a human being lies in your resistance to evil. We fight, therefore we are!*
>
> —MENACHEM BEGIN
> on the necessity of
> armed resistance

Another ship, the S.S. *Struma*, carrying more than 750 people on a vessel normally suited for about 100, sank off the coast of Istanbul after months in immigration limbo. After this incident, placards appeared throughout Palestine reading, in Hebrew and English: "Wanted for murder! Sir Harold MacMichael, known as the high commissioner for Palestine, wanted for murder by drowning of 800 refugees aboard the S.S. *Struma*."

It was into this charged atmosphere that Menachem Begin had arrived. It was only a matter of time before he became involved with the *Irgun Z'vai Leumi* (National Military Organization), the underground group that put military force and action behind the words and ideas of Vladimir Jabotinsky.

Like the Revisionists in Europe, the Irgun represented a minority viewpoint. It was one of several Zionist military organizations in Palestine. The *Haganah* was the primary security force and was subject to the authority of the Jewish Agency, which was the main representative of the Zionist establishment in Palestine. The Haganah followed a general policy of *havlagah*, or restraint, which meant that it was a defensive force to be used only if Jews or their property were attacked. This was the theory developed by leaders such as Chaim Weizmann and David Ben-Gurion, who favored negotiations with the British and opposed antagonizing the Arabs and jeopardizing innocent lives. In addition, Weizmann and his colleagues did not want to rule out eventual coexistence with the Arabs.

The Irgun, in contrast, strongly disagreed with Haganah's defensive character and believed instead in an aggressive approach to the British and the Arabs. The Irgun advocated active opposition to the British rule in Palestine, although they agreed to cease anti-British activities for the duration of the war. Its philosophy of armed power and displays of force were thoroughly in keeping with Jabotinsky's position, but it was condemned by the Jewish Agency and most of the *yishuv*, the Jewish community in Palestine. A particular point of disagreement was that the Irgun did not help establish such necessary institutions as settlements, hospitals,

and service agencies for the future Jewish state but concentrated mainly on waging war.

Begin found the Irgun in disarray. Jabotinsky was dead. So was David Raziel, an inspiring Irgun commander who had been killed in 1941 while helping the British on an undercover mission in Iraq. Avraham Stern, a militant who found the Irgun policy of cooperation with the British during the early days of World War II too cautious, had broken with his comrades in 1940 to form a new group, the *Lohamei Herut Israel* (Fighters for Freedom of Israel), known by the Hebrew acronym of *Lehi* and to English speakers as the Stern Gang. (Stern was killed by the British in 1942, but the group remained intact.) In addition, the British had campaigned actively against the Irgun, imprisoning its members and confiscating arms and printing presses, so that mounting any significant operations or publicizing its program was made extremely difficult. What the Irgun needed was Begin — his charisma and his knack for making things happen.

British police halt a march of Jews protesting the White Paper of 1939. The document set a quota on Jewish immigration to Palestine, which was to be stopped completely by 1944, and restricted Jewish purchases of land owned by Arabs.

A section of the city of Jaffa, sealed off with barbed wire and guarded by British soldiers, awaits detonation. To control the rioting that was resulting in the deaths of both Jews and Arabs, the British resorted to destroying the places they believed sheltered the instigators.

The 30-year-old Begin was a rebel and a nonconformist, a man of considerable will who was not easily distracted from his objectives. Although he had little military training and was a lawyer and a Biblical scholar with no experience in underground conspiracy, he was well known as an orator, a patriot, and a highly skilled organizer. He would be perfect for the enormous task that lay ahead.

At the Battle of El Alamein in Egypt in October 1942, German and Italian forces were defeated by Allied troops commanded by British general Bernard Montgomery. It was a turning point in the war, marking the beginning of the end of German domination of North Africa and removing the immediate Axis threat to the Middle East. As an Allied victory in the war became more apparent over the course of the following year, Revisionist Zionist leaders in Palestine decided the time was right to step up attacks against the British. At the end of 1943, having obtained a discharge from the Polish army, Begin took command of the Irgun. "In this new chapter [of my life]," Begin observed later, "fate played another of its tricks on me. Conspiratorial work was to me quite unknown before I plunged . . . into its depths. I knew nothing of underground activities, beyond what I had read in an occasional book. I had never dreamt I would fight underground. In all things I always preferred the open to the secret, and yet . . . . "

On February 1, 1944, he issued the group's call to arms, a "proclamation of revolt" announcing the end of the Irgun "armistice" with Britain. The proclamation outlined the reasons for the Jewish resentment of Britain. Jews in Palestine had freely supported the Allies against Germany. Many had volunteered to fight with the British, while many Arabs supported the Germans. In repayment, the British had prevented those Jews who had managed to escape the Nazi horrors from settling in Palestine. Addressed to the British, it read, in part:

"There is no longer any armistice between the Jewish people and the British administration in Eretz Israel [Land of Israel] which hands our brothers over to Hitler. Our people are at war with this regime —war to the end.

"This war will demand many and heavy sacrifices, but we enter on it in the consciousness that we are being faithful to the children of our people who have been and are being slaughtered. It is for their sake that we fight, to their dying testimony that we remain loyal.

"This, then is our demand: immediate transfer of power in Eretz Israel to a provisional Hebrew government."

This poster clearly indicates the methods the _Irgun Z'vai Leumi_ advocated to acquire control of Palestine. Shortly after his arrival in the country, Begin joined the Irgun, which followed Jabotinsky's militant Zionism. By the end of 1943 Begin commanded the underground organization.

6

The Revolt

The question of whether Menachem Begin was a "freedom fighter," along the lines of Garibaldi, the 19th-century Italian patriot and soldier, or a "terrorist" hung over the Irgun leader throughout the Jews' struggle for statehood. The importance of the question is clear. Terrorists are generally regarded as criminals, degraders of human life, while freedom fighters are popular heroes. The distinction is often a matter of interpretation; one person's freedom fighter is another's terrorist. Walter Laquer, the author of the book *Terrorism* and an expert on Middle East affairs, has written that "Terrorism, broadly speaking, can be considered the use of violence, usually by a small group of people, for political ends." More important, he points out, "It is not always unjustified."

Not surprisingly, Menachem Begin has had something to say on the matter as well. In his account of the Jews' fight for independence, *The Revolt*, he wrote: "The underground fighters of the Irgun arose to overthrow and replace a regime. We used physical force because we were faced by physical force. But physical force was neither our aim nor our creed. We believed in the supremacy of moral forces. . . . Our purpose, in fact, was precisely the reverse of 'terrorism.' The whole essence of our struggle was the determination to free our people of its chief affliction — fear. How could we continue to live in this hostile world in which the Jew was attacked because he was a Jew — how could we go on living without

There is no other way apart from a war of liberation.
—MENACHEM BEGIN

British officials view a government complex in Jerusalem damaged by a terrorist bombing in which three British policemen were killed. Begin's Irgunists launched a steady stream of violent acts against the British to force them out of Palestine.

arms, without a homeland, without elementary means of defense? We of the Irgun Z'vai Leumi arose therefore to rebel and fight, not in order to instill fear but to eradicate it. . . . We were not 'terrorists.' We were strictly speaking antiterrorists. . . . We created no group of assassins to lurk in wait for important victims."

Many disagreed with Begin's views and with his distinctions, but there is little doubt his tactics had an effect. Israeli historian Michael J. Cohen wrote that "history would seem to indicate that the IZL's [Irgun Z'vai Leumi's] draconian methods, morally reprehensible as they were, were decisive" in getting the British to give up the mandate.

The Irgun went into action against the British in February 1944, shortly after Begin's call to arms. Over the next several months its 600 fighters bombed immigration, tax, and police offices in Jerusalem, Tel Aviv, and Haifa, stole arms from a British camp, and even stole money from fellow Jews in order to fund their campaign. Both the Irgun and the British suffered casualties along the way.

As a new revolutionary, Begin learned fast. One of his operations chiefs later recalled that "Begin wanted targets that would make a great impact in the world. Sometimes he wanted us to stop actions. What I admired about Begin was his analytical mind, his political analysis. It helped to convince me of the possibilities of our war, of the future."

The revolt sparked harsh retaliatory measures by the British. Among these was the mass roundup, detention, and deportation of Irgunists. Some 250 Irgun and Lehi fighters were sent to an East African prisoner-of-war camp, a severe blow to both organizations. A substantial reward was offered by the British for Begin's capture.

The Irgun also incurred the wrath of Ben-Gurion and the Zionist establishment, who called them "maniacs, bandits, and nihilists" who "stabbed Zionism in the back" by not following the path of political negotiation. Pressure mounted on Ben-Gurion to crack down on the militants. In late October 1944 his representatives urged Begin to cease his activities, stressing that Britain would change its policies once World War II ended. When Begin

Begin and Aliza with their son Binyamin Ze'ev, 1945. During his years with the Irgun, Begin assumed several disguises and aliases and regularly had to move his family to avoid capture by the British authorities.

refused, one of the Haganah men said plainly, "We shall step in and finish you." Begin grew depressed, convinced that what he feared most was about to happen—civil war among the Jews.

The situation deteriorated still further. On November 6, in Cairo, two young Lehi members murdered Lord Moyne (Walter Edward Guinness), England's minister for Middle East affairs and a close friend of British prime minister Winston Churchill. The assassination caused an uproar in England and even prompted Chaim Weizmann to say that the shock of Moyne's death had been "far more severe and numbing than that of the death of my own son." *Haaretz*, the influential Jewish newspaper in Palestine, wrote, "Since Zionism began, no more grievous blow has been struck at our cause."

The Irgun paid heavily for the crime. The Jewish Agency issued a statement saying that "The yishuv is required to spew up all members of this destructive and ruinous gang, to deny them shelter and refuge, not to give in to their threats and to grant the authorities all the aid required to prevent the acts of terror and liquidate its organization, for our lives depend on it." What became know as the *saison*, or the hunting season, began; its goal was to destroy the Irgun. The Haganah hunted and arrested Irgunists throughout Palestine and gave names of Irgunists and their supporters to the British authorities. For seven months the saison continued, but ultimately the Jewish Agency came to view the Moyne assassination as a "bitter and tragic necessity." For their cooperation with the British the Jewish Agency received no reward — no relaxation in immigration laws and no further support for a homeland. Worse, the fratricidal atmosphere of the saison left scars on all involved and worsened an already bad situation.

The Irgun gained and lost from the saison. It suffered a terrible loss in personnel and maneuverability. On the positive side there was not a single instance of an Irgunist retaliating against any of the Jews who campaigned against them; this restraint was noted by the yishuv. In November 1944 Begin had instructed his men, in part, as follows: "Do not raise a hand and do not use arms against Hebrew youths. They are not responsible. They are our brothers. They are being misdirected and incited. But the day will come when they will realize their error and fight side by side with us against the foreign oppression."

The Irgun also gained a bit of sympathy for being something of an underdog. Amazingly, Begin managed to remain at large all the while, free to continue masterminding the struggle.

Begin's strategies for staying in the shadows throughout the revolt were brilliant. He assumed a number of aliases and kept moving about the Tel Aviv area in order to avoid capture by the British. His first refuge was the Savoy Hotel, where he lived as "Menachem Ben-Ze'ev," Ze'ev being Jabotinsky's Hebrew name. Next, he and Aliza moved to Petach Tikva, a city east of Tel Aviv, and stayed for a time in a section that was home to immigrants from Yemen. Begin's light complexion did not allow him to blend in with the mostly dark-skinned Yemenites, so he and Aliza moved to a different quarter of the town, where he adopted the name Yisrael Halperin and introduced himself to neighbors as an immigrant from Poland.

His next stop was Tel Aviv itself, where he became the bearded Orthodox Jew, Yisrael Sassover. (The beard added years to his appearance.) Part of his role playing there included frequent prayer at the local synagogue. The birth of the Begins' second child, a daughter named Hassia (after Menachem's mother), provided additional camouflage — the British were on the lookout for a man with a wife and one child, a boy. Begin's final disguise was as Dr. Yonah Koenigshoffer, a name taken from an identity card that had found its way into Irgun hands. For this role Begin trimmed his facial hair back to a mustache, since the Haganah had found out about his beard.

Begin was fond of saying that he was living in the "open underground." He and the Irgunists exposed themselves, he explained, "as a means of hiding more effectively. We assumed that it would not occur to the authorities that the chief terrorist lived in a place where everybody knew his neighbors. We were not mistaken." The British did conduct mass searches of the various neighborhoods in which Begin lived, however. On one occasion he had to hide in a special cubbyhole in his home for four stifling days and nights. On another, he and a friend were able to sit on the front steps of their home and watch the British go about their business. The police pressure inhibited Aliza's movements as well. When her father died, she could not attend the funeral or burial, for the British knew of the familial connections and watched the rites, hoping for the chance to follow Aliza home.

As the British and the Haganah gradually lost their appetite for the hunt and World War II came to an end, attention shifted to the British election of July 1945. Britain's Labour Party had earlier promised a "fair deal" to its Labor Zionist brothers in Palestine and had announced at a preelection conference in Blackpool that the terms of the 1939 White Paper would be rescinded and that the party supported the creation of a Jewish state in Palestine.

Churchill and the Conservatives, meanwhile, continued to place greater importance on cultivating Arab good will and were still smarting from the Moyne assassination. When Labour won and the Conservatives were forced to step down, the Zionists rejoiced, saying the election marked "a clear victory for the demands of Zionism."

> *Our people is at war with this regime—war to the end. There will be no retreat. Freedom—or Death!*
>
> —Proclamation of the Irgun Z'vai Leumi, declaring rebellion against British occupation, 1943

But within weeks of the change in government it became apparent that the Labour Party was capable of giving only lukewarm support to the Zionist movement. The White Paper remained intact, even as the full extent of the Nazi Holocaust was becoming known throughout the world. The new foreign secretary, Ernest Bevin, offended many by making a series of statements that appeared to make light of the Jews' suffering. Because Bevin and the new prime minister, Clement Attlee, could not deliver what the Zionists had been led to expect, Weizmann's entire cooperative approach to the British lost its credibility. Ben-Gurion, frustrated and disappointed by this turn of events, concluded that diplomacy might have run its course. "The acts of the British government are a continuation of Hitler's policy of hostility," he said — a comment the outcast Begin might well have made. More astounding still was what Ben-Gurion did next. He turned to the militant Irgun and Lehi and asked them to join the Haganah in forming a united resistance movement.

After the three groups had agreed to act in close concert with one another — but not to merge their forces — the coalition, called the Hebrew Resistance Movement, swung into action in the autumn with attacks against railway installations and British police targets. The groups also raided British stores of arms, destroyed planes belonging to the Royal Air Force, and blew up the bridges connecting Palestine to its neighbors. By mid-1946 Palestine had become an armed camp, complete with bunkers, sandbags, motorized patrols, and 100,000 British soldiers and policemen. Yet the resistance, made up of just 5,000 fighters, held the British in check — and then some. As J. Bowyer Bell wrote in *Terror Out of Zion*, "The mandate became a garrison state under internal siege, and the garrison [military installation], despite its size, equipment, and determination, proved ineffectual and self-defeating."

On Saturday, June 29, the British began their most forceful and effective response — an operation that came to be known as Black Sabbath. Nearly 3,000 Jews were detained, among them some of the

movement's leaders, and a curfew was put in place. British soldiers swooped down upon Tel Aviv, searching block by block and house to house for arms and for resistance fighters in hiding. Begin and the Irgun responded with the most violent attack ever aimed at the British in Palestine.

The British "nerve center" in Palestine, the headquarters of their administration, was the King David Hotel in Jerusalem, a luxury establishment overlooking the Old City. On July 22, 1946, 350 kilograms of dynamite exploded in the hotel, demolishing much of it and killing 91 people — 28 Britons, 41 Arabs, 17 Jews, 2 Armenians, 1 Russian, 1 Greek, and 1 Egyptian. The operation, carried out by the Irgun with at least initial support from the Haganah, had been planned as a symbolic attack on British prestige, not one that would claim so many casualties. Shortly before the blast, an Irgun woman had notified the King David's switchboard, the Palestine *Post*, and the French consulate across the street that the hotel had been mined and that an explosion was soon to occur. To this day it is not clear why the premises were not evacuated, unless, simply, the warnings were issued too late. The bombing, which has been called a "tragedy of er-

The King David Hotel in Jerusalem housed the administrative offices of the British forces in Palestine. In July 1946 the Irgun bombed the hotel, killing nearly 100 people, and was severely condemned for the cold-blooded action.

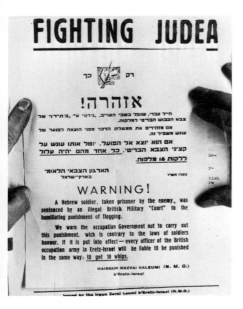

In this 1946 circular mailed to the British press in England, the Irgun warns that it will respond to British actions against captured Irgunists by kidnapping British officers and delivering the same "humiliating" punishment they meted out: flogging.

rors," remains one of the most controversial incidents in Israel's history. Its most immediate effect was to spell the end of the united resistance movement.

The day after the bombing, the Haganah issued a public statement: "The Hebrew Resistance Movement denounces the heavy toll of lives caused in the dissidents' operation at the King David Hotel." The Haganah had returned to its old view of the Irgun as a renegade band of terrorists. Although the operation had been planned with the Haganah, the group had repeatedly asked for postponements, and Weizmann, who was keeping up his diplomatic efforts, had flatly forbidden any such actions. Amid the confusion of a movement still suspicious of one another's motives, the Irgun went ahead. Begin was condemned by the world press, and British hostility to the Jews increased, as the entire Jewish community was punished for the bombing. A strict curfew was imposed on Tel Aviv and Jerusalem, and British troops in both cities had orders to shoot any violators on the spot. Jewish homes and shops were declared off limits to British soldiers and all contact was forbidden.

Begin, though he was in one of his disguises, could not risk relying on his cover as "Rabbi Sassover" and remained for four days and four nights in the summer heat without food or water in a hidden cupboard that a friend had built in his apartment for this sort of emergency. Aliza could not risk opening the cupboard door to pass in food or water. British soldiers, informed that the "rabbi" had gone to Jerusalem, were waiting under the windows of the first-floor apartment for him to return; several times soldiers had walked in unannounced to ask for a drink, and if they or even one of her own small children were to see Aliza opening the secret door, all would be lost. When the British finally left after their four-day vigil, Begin was barely conscious.

In the churning aftermath of the bombing, one thing was clear: the operation had at least partly achieved its desired objective: the British realized that there was no avoiding the fact that its presence in Palestine was becoming more trouble than it was worth.

In the fall the Irgun resumed its anti-British activities. The British response this time was more severe punishment of Irgunists who had been caught and found guilty of violating the mandate's laws — the offenders were flogged and sometimes hanged. After one young Irgunist was given 18 strokes with a cane, four Britons were kidnapped by the Irgun and repaid in kind. As Gervasi points out, however, Begin's reaction was not simply "an eye for an eye" retaliation; rather, it revealed his "fierce devotion to the sanctity of his fellow Jews as human beings. What ever happened to them happened to [Begin] personally."

The British, warned by the Irgun that the tit-for-tat would continue, put an end to the floggings. Begin, who had seen Jews whipped in Poland, said of the exchange, "Our brother Jews throughout the world straightened their backs. After generations of humiliation by whipping, they had witnessed an episode which restored their dignity and self-respect."

That new sense of pride was evident in April 1947, after the British ordered that an Irgunist named Dov Gruner be hung in the fortress prison where he was being held in the town of Acre, on the Mediterranean Sea. Another Jewish prisoner later reported that

In a daring raid, the Irgun in May 1947 blasted through a wall in the British fortress prison at Acre, freeing hundreds of prisoners. It was an exhilarating victory for Begin, who compared the mission to the capture of the Bastille during the French Revolution of 1789.

Gruner sang the Zionist anthem, "Hatikvah" (The Hope), as he was led to his death. Two more Irgunists were to be executed days later, but rather than submit to British justice they detonated a homemade grenade to end their lives before the sentence could be carried out. The incident shocked the British and so inspired the Irgunists that they went on to one of the greatest successes of their entire revolt.

The fortress in Acre had been built by the Crusaders hundreds of years earlier and was still considered impenetrable. The British used it to hold both Jewish and Arab prisoners. The Irgun came up with the audacious idea of breaking into the prison and freeing the Jews being held there. Disguising themselves as Arabs, several Irgunists scouted the outside of the structure and the maze-like town that surrounded it, mapping approaches and escape routes. Inside, a stealthy Irgunist discovered a weak spot in one of the fortress's storage rooms. After piecing all the information together, a plan was ready. On May 4, 1947, an explosion blasted a hole in the prison wall, through which 251 inmates escaped, about half of them Jewish. Though mistakes and fighting outside the prison led to 15 Jewish deaths and the capture of several escapees, the mission was a success overall. Begin likened it to the famous storming of the Bastille fortress in Paris during the French Revolution of 1789.

In June three of the Jews captured during the breakout were sentenced by the British to hang. The Irgun responded by abducting and threatening to hang two British sergeants (Begin had hoped to nab higher-ranking officials). The following month both sides carried out the sentences. Again Begin was condemned throughout the world. In England anti-Semitic riots erupted in London, Manchester, Liverpool, and Glasgow. In Palestine the Jewish Agency declared, "It is mortifying that some Jews should have become so depraved by the horrible iniquities in Europe as to be capable of such vileness." Begin later wrote, "[Our enemy] . . . forced us to answer gallows with gallows. But the days were as black as starless nights."

British tanks maintain an uneasy peace in the streets of Jerusalem, May 1948, four days before the mandate expired. The United States, which feared the outbreak of a war between the Jews and the Palestinian Arabs once the British left, urged both sides to accept a truce until an acceptable political solution could be reached.

The British carried out no more executions of Jews. Perhaps more important, the episode forced the British government to examine, once and for all, its position in Palestine. Following the hangings, a Labour cabinet minister wrote to Prime Minister Attlee: "The time has almost come when we might bring our troops out of Palestine altogether. The present state of affairs is not only costly to us in manpower and money, but is, as you and I agree, of no real value from the strategic point of view — you cannot in any case have a secure base on top of a wasps' nest — and it is exposing our young men, for no good purpose, to most abominable experience, and is breeding anti-Semites at a most shocking speed."

Earlier in the year Britain had pronounced the mandate "unworkable," sought United Nations help in finding a political solution, and announced their intention to withdraw from Palestine on May 15, 1948. The time for UN action had arrived.

7

A State Is Born

At its height in Biblical times, the Jewish empire encompassed the hill country of Judea and Samaria, the Negev Desert, the Sea of Galilee, the Plain of Sharon along the Mediterranean, land extending east across the Jordan River and Jerusalem. The Palestine over which Britain assumed control after World War I resembled, for the most part, this configuration. In 1922 Winston Churchill, then Britain's colonial secretary, established the Emir Abdullah, a Bedouin chieftain from northwestern Saudi Arabia, as the administrator of all the lands east of the Jordan, then known as the Transjordan. This was done to prevent Abdullah from marching on Syria to claim the throne there, which would have caused problems between Britain and France, which controlled Syria. According to an English statesman involved in the affair, Transjordan was "intended to serve as a reserve of land for use in the resettlement of Arabs once the national Home for the Jews in Palestine . . . became an accomplished fact. There was no intention at that stage of forming territory east of the river Jordan into an independent Arab state."

But that is precisely what happened. Transjordan, which constituted roughly 80 percent of the mandate, became the British-sanctioned Kingdom of Transjordan in 1946. Thus, discussions over the establishment of a Jewish state necessarily focused on the land west of the Jordan River.

A regime resting on a thousand bayonets had collapsed; and in its place . . . a very old nation was being reborn.
—MENACHEM BEGIN
on the establishment of the
state of Israel in 1948

Begin, the *Herut* party candidate for prime minister, casts his vote in the 1949 election. When Begin turned from underground activity to politics, his hard-line views made him the natural leader of the right-wing nationalists and the opponent of the ruling Labor Zionists.

Three Israeli soldiers walk through the ruins of an Arab city in May 1948. When the British withdrew from the country, a guerrilla war erupted between the Jews and Arabs in Palestine, each side intent on claiming power for itself.

In November 1947 the United Nations General Assembly decided to "partition" that land into a Jewish state and an Arab state. According to Israeli journalist Amos Elon, "The basic premise underlying the decision was that two intense nationalisms had clashed over Palestine. Both possessed validity and yet were totally irreconcilable. Regardless of the historical origins of the conflict, the rights and wrongs of the promises and counter-promises, the basic fact was the presence in the country of 650,000 Jews and 1,220,000 Arabs."

Weizmann, Ben-Gurion, and the mainstream Zionists reluctantly supported the partition plan. They reasoned that even a partitioned homeland was preferable to continued uncertainty and violence. Said one Zionist spokesperson, "This sacrifice would be the Jewish contribution to the solution of a painful problem and would bear witness to the Jewish people's spirit of international cooperation and its desire for peace."

Begin was vehemently opposed to the plan. He wanted the whole of Palestine, for spiritual and practical reasons. In a spiritual sense, he felt that the Jewish land was indivisible; in practical terms, he was convinced, the United Nations plan was impossible. Jerusalem would be completely surrounded by Arab territory, and the two antagonists would be "entwined in an inimical embrace like two

UPI/BETTMANN NEWSPHOTOS

Prime Minister David Ben-Gurion announces the creation of the new nation of Israel, May 14, 1948. Begin felt that Ben-Gurion had compromised too much when he accepted the UN partition plan, which attempted to solve the Palestinian problem by creating in Palestine two separate states — one Jewish, the other Arab.

fighting pythons each bent on swallowing the other," as one writer put it.

When the partition agreement was adopted, with Zionist approval, the Irgun issued a warning: "The partition of the homeland is illegal. It will never be recognized. The signature by institutions and individuals of the partitions agreement is invalid. It will not bind the Jewish people. Jerusalem was and will forever be our capital. Eretz Israel will be restored to the people of Israel. All of it. And forever." But the Irgunists were a distinct minority, and the Jews in Palestine danced in the streets in celebration. Independence was near. The mandate was slated to end on May 15, 1948.

The Arabs also objected to the partition plan and urged a united Arab effort to exterminate the Jews in Palestine. Palestine was theirs and had been for years, they believed, and they resented a settlement being forced upon them. Why did European guilt over the treatment of the Jews in World War II have to be soothed in the Middle East? they asked. As the British began to withdraw, Arabs from the surrounding nations began to infiltrate Palestine. A guerrilla war between Jews and Arabs broke out, with a larger war seeming imminent as the days of the mandate dwindled down.

In April 1948, with the two sides jockeying for control of key roads and villages in preparation for

an all-out struggle, the Irgun planned an operation against Deir Yassin, an Arab village of 800 to 1,000 people. Deir Yassin was strategically located on the sole road connecting Jerusalem with western Palestine. The Arabs sought to blockade Jerusalem, isolating the 100,000 Jews in the city from their countrymen. Some analysts, reviewing the eventual attack on Deir Yassin, say the Irgun sought to seize control of the village for this reason. The Haganah agreed that the city would have to be captured at some point and also wanted to build an airstrip for contact with the coast. Other historians say the Irgun wanted to show that it was more than a band of terrorists, that it could pull off more sophisticated operations. Still others say that the attack was planned as revenge for the Arab conquest of two Jewish settlements near Jerusalem and that it was also intended to spark fear among Arabs elsewhere in Palestine, fear that would make them flee. The Haganah approved the raid only reluctantly, for it believed more important targets lay near Jerusalem but did not wish to risk more strife among Jews by arguing the point.

The raid, by 80 Irgunists and 40 Stern Gang members, turned into a horrible massacre. No warning was given, and about 120 people — some say 250 — were slaughtered, including many old men, women, and children. It was the frenzy of the killings, not the numbers, that made Deir Yassin a singular event. Eric Silver relates that the Irgun and the Sternists shot at anything that moved and blew up houses with people inside. Begin later wrote that when the Zionists subsequently captured Haifa and other villages near Jerusalem, the Arabs fled in terror, shouting "Deir Yassin." To this day Deir Yassin is cited by the Arab world as an example of an atrocity committed by the Jews against the Arabs, an instance of "Zionist terrorism." Though a legend has grown up around the affair that seems to exceed by far what went on there, it remains one of the most infamous episodes in Israel's history.

Later in the month Begin and the Irgunists redeemed themselves to a degree by leading the daring capture of Jaffa.

On May 14, 1948, the British high commissioner for Palestine departed, formally ending Britain's involvement in the country. That night, Ben-Gurion, speaking for the executive committee of the Jewish Agency and the Jewish National Council, proclaimed the establishment of the state of Israel, effective the next day. On May 15 Begin spoke to the country in a radio address: "The Irgun Z'vai Leumi is leaving the underground within the boundaries of the independent Hebrew state. We went down into the underground, we arose in the underground under the rule of oppression. Now, we have Hebrew rule in part of our homeland. In this part there is no need for a Hebrew underground. In the state of Israel we shall be soldiers and builders. We shall respect its government, for it is our government."

Only in Jerusalem did the Irgunists hold out. Begin suspected that Ben-Gurion would not try to capture the entire city, and he wanted the Irgun to be poised to do so.

Meanwhile, the Arab armies of Egypt, Syria, Iraq, Transjordan, and Lebanon, with contingents from Saudi Arabia, Sudan, and Yemen, invaded Israel in an attempt to destroy the Jewish state, to "drive the Jews into the sea," as their propaganda said. The war raged on into June. Tel Aviv and Jerusalem were threatened, and Transjordan's British-trained, well-armed Arab Legion had occupied much of Judea and Samaria — the West Bank of the Jordan River. The Jews were desperately short of arms and ammunition. With that in mind, Begin and the Irgun, with American and French support, sought to put together a shipment of arms and personnel to use them. On June 11 a UN-mediated cease-fire between the Jews and the Arabs went into effect. That same day, the *Altalena*, a ship carrying $5 million worth of arms and hundreds of willing fighters, left its port in France for Israel.

Begin viewed the arms and manpower aboard the *Altalena* as vital to the war effort, enough perhaps to overrun the Arab armies. Ben-Gurion recognized the need for arms but also saw the shipment as a challenge to his authority. Despite the official policy of cooperation, the Irgun (and the Lehi) and the

The moment the state came into being, it was assumed that the Irgun would submit to the jurisdiction of the Israeli government. . . . This could only be viewed as an irresponsible and wanton defiance of government authority and had to be vigorously and speedily dealt with.
—MOSHE DAYAN
Israeli general and cabinet minister, on the *Altalena* incident

AP/WIDE WORLD PHOTOS

Soldiers of the Israeli army collect guns and ammunition from the Irgun. Responding to an ultimatum from Ben-Gurion to disarm, Begin finally ordered his Irgunists to obey and thus avoided a potentially disastrous Jewish civil war.

Haganah continued to fight separately from one another, the Irgun taking its orders from Begin and the Haganah obeying the newly formed provisional government under Ben-Gurion. Still suspicious of the Irgun, Ben-Gurion thought Begin might try to make a grab for power. Begin had opposed the partition plan, and Ben-Gurion thought he had better be wary.

As the boat approached Israel, suspicions mounted as the government and the Irgun discussed whether it should land, who should unload the arms, and how the arms should be distributed. From Ben-Gurion's point of view, it looked as if Begin wanted to maintain a private army. He said, "There are not going to be two states, and there are not going to be two armies. And Mr. Begin will not do whatever he feels like. We must decide to hand over power to Begin or to tell him to cease his separatist activities. If he does not give in, we shall open fire."

The boat landed north of Tel Aviv on the evening of June 20. Begin boarded the vessel, and the Irgun began unloading the arms. After Begin refused an ultimatum to turn over the arms to the Israel Defense Forces (IDF), the new state's army, fighting broke out. The matériel was reloaded and the boat moved on to Tel Aviv. The standoff continued the next day. Ultimately, Ben-Gurion ordered that the ship be fired upon, and it was soon set ablaze. Begin abandoned the vessel, narrowly escaping death. In the skirmishing that occurred as the ship sank, 14 Irgunists were killed, 69 were wounded, and much of the arms were lost. Addressing the nation later by radio, Begin called Ben-Gurion "that fool, that idiot," and a "crazy dictator." He wept in public, taboo for political leaders the world over. Ben-Gurion had thus averted a civil war and succeeded in humiliating and eliminating his main political opposition. It was an ugly affair on all sides.

It was said later that with the arms and fighters aboard the *Altalena*, the IDF might have been able to capture Judea, Samaria, and the Old City of Jerusalem. Instead, the frontiers of Israel that emerged after the signing of armistice agreements in 1949 left those lands in Arab hands. Though Israel had more land, with more secure borders, than had been allowed for in the partition plan, Begin was not satisfied. He wanted Jewish sovereignty over the entire homeland. He turned to politics to finish his task.

Officials hoist the flag of the new state of Israel, May 15, 1948. The joy felt at the momentous occasion was tempered for many by the fear that their fledgling nation, surrounded by hostile Arab countries, would have to keep fighting to survive.

8

The Loyal Opposition

The name Begin gave to the political party he led into the new state of Israel's first elections in January 1949 was *Herut*, Hebrew for freedom. To gain a seat in the 120-member parliament, which was officially named the *Knesset* shortly thereafter, it was necessary to win at least 1 percent of the total votes cast. Herut won 14 seats, making it the third largest single party in the country, but leaving it far behind Ben-Gurion's *Mapai*, the Israel Workers party, which captured 46 seats and by forming a coalition with other, smaller parties was able to form a government with Ben-Gurion as prime minister. In the 1951 elections Herut had only eight seats, and the pattern was set: Begin was the odd man out in Israeli politics. This does not mean that he disappeared — far from it. Rather, as Israel's citizens continued the immense task of building their new nation, Begin found himself speaking on a number of important issues from a position of opposition to the government.

In the early 1950s Begin led a campaign against Israel's acceptance of German war reparations — money paid by losers in wars to compensate the victims. Israelis found the issue quite troublesome. Many thought that no price could be put on the losses suffered in the Holocaust. Also, they were afraid that if Israel accepted the payments, the Germans might seem to have "bought" their way out

> *Menachem Begin as a politician has been guided by the premonition of a world rising up to destroy Israel.*
> —EITAN HABER
> Israeli journalist

Begin, leader of the "loyal opposition," makes a speech before an attentive crowd in 1954. For over two decades after Israeli independence was declared, Begin held to a strong nationalist line, advocating the conquest and colonization of territory, including the Old City of Jerusalem, the Gaza Strip, and the West Bank.

of guilt and responsibility for the horrors they had caused. Ben-Gurion had sought reparations from Chancellor Konrad Adenauer of West Germany (Germany was partitioned into two nations, East Germany and West Germany, after World War II), saying the funds were needed to prop up the desperately troubled Israeli economy. Begin, of course, was outraged.

Taking to the streets on January 7, 1952, he addressed a Jerusalem crowd: "Today the Jewish premier is about to announce that he will go to Germany to receive money, that he will sell the honor of the Jewish people for monetary gain, casting eternal shame upon it. . . . There is not one German who did not murder our parents. Every Ger-

Israelis protest the arrival of the first German ambassador to their country, 1965. In the early 1950s Begin had opposed Ben-Gurion's acceptance of German reparations payments, arguing that no amount of money could compensate the Holocaust survivors or reduce the guilt of the German people.

man is a Nazi. Every German is a murderer. Adenauer is a murderer. All his aides are murderers. But their reckoning is money, money, money. This abomination will be perpetrated for a few million dollars." He then led a march on the Knesset building, which soon turned violent. According to the Jerusalem *Post*, "Police barbed-wire barricades were broken through, parked cars overturned, and rocks thrown into the Knesset chamber and at police protecting the building. Injuries had reached ninety-two policemen and thirty-six civilians by 7:00 P.M. when an army detachment arrived on the scene in formation alongside the Knesset. By 7:30 order had been restored." Meanwhile, inside the Knesset the debate had been joined. After Begin read a list of prominent Israelis who opposed reparations, Ben-Gurion said, "They are not identified with your fascist hooligans in the street."

"You are the fascist hooligan," Begin replied, causing an uproar. Ben-Gurion eventually carried the vote in parliament, however, and an agreement was signed by which Germany provided more than $800 million worth of funds, goods, and services to Israel and to Jews in other countries.

Four years later, in late 1956, Israel, with help from Great Britain and France, captured the Sinai

Begin addresses members of the Knesset, the Israeli parliament, including Ben-Gurion (center foreground) and Golda Meir. After the dismal showing of his Herut party in the 1961 elections, Begin engineered a new coalition party, called *Gahal*. However, Ben-Gurion's Labor candidates continued to dominate.

Peninsula from Egypt. Israel's attack was primarily a reaction to repeated acts of Arab terrorism and provocation and was aimed at creating a "buffer zone" between Egypt and Israel's major population centers. The British and French assisted Israel because they hoped to regain control of the Suez Canal, the vital waterway connecting the Mediterranean Sea and the Red Sea. Much of the two countries' shipping passed through the Canal. President Gamal Abdel Nasser of Egypt had nationalized the canal earlier in the year. Begin backed the attack as a proper "preventive" measure, and when Israel withdrew its troops from the area in 1957 under strong international pressure, he criticized Ben-Gurion for "selling away" the country's security.

Begin subsequently faced a challenge to his continued leadership of Herut. Though the political party had revived in the 1955 elections, winning 15 seats, it gained only two seats in the 1959 election and two in 1961. The numbers were disappointing. Begin then forged an alliance with the Liberal party to form *Gahal* (which stands for Gush-Herut-Liberalism, or a block of Herut and the Liberals). Gahal appeared to represent a significant alternative to the continued dominance of Mapai and its allied parties, also known as the Labor alignment. Unfortunately, Gahal won only 26 seats in the 1965 elections — one fewer than the total number held by Herut and the Liberals before the two merged.

Rumblings of discontent erupted at the Herut convention the following year. One young Herut dissident told the assembled coalition members that, "Up to now Begin has led the movement as an opposition to the ruling regime, but he has not succeeded in leading it to rule. He must accept the consequences and resign together with the entire leadership." Begin held his ground, and Gahal remained intact. Then another crisis came to the fore, this one threatening the entire country.

"We intend to open a general assault against Israel. This will be total war. Our basic aim is the destruction of Israel." So spoke Egypt's Nasser in late May 1967, as Egypt, Syria, and Jordan prepared their latest concerted effort against the ·Jewish

> *A State? No. We cannot recognize that. A Jewish people, a nonpolitical community, yes. But not a state.*
> —GAMAL ABDEL NASSER
> Egyptian premier, 1967

state. Nasser had made war virtually inevitable by forcing the removal of United Nations peacekeeping forces from the Sinai Peninsula, moving Egyptian forces and armaments into the area, and blockading the Gulf of Aqaba and the Strait of Tiran, Israel's outlets to the Red Sea and beyond.

To deal with the menace, a government of national unity was formed, a broad-based coalition that would permit wide support for the kinds of stringent measures often required in wartime. Dissatisfied with what he perceived as the hesitant leadership of Prime Minister Levi Eshkol, who had replaced Ben-Gurion as Prime minister in 1963, Begin recommended that Eshkol resign and allow Ben-Gurion to head the unity government. Unaware that the aging Ben-Gurion (now 80) opposed war with Egypt, Begin felt that only his old rival was decisive enough and commanded sufficient popular support to govern. When Eshkol refused to step down, Begin insisted that Moshe Dayan, the colorful and dynamic sabra who had served brilliantly as chief of staff during the Sinai campaign, be named defense minister. Eshkol agreed and also named Begin to serve as a cabinet minister within the unity government.

Gervasi describes Begin's actions just before he officially joined the new cabinet: "Early the next morning, on his way to the swearing-in ceremony at the Knesset, Begin had his driver stop at Mount Herzl so that he could pay his respects at the grave of Vladimir Jabotinsky. The gesture was characteristic of Begin, whose emotions run deep. Before taking his oath of office, he wished to commune with the spirit of his mentor, the man he calls 'my master.'

"Begin stood at the foot of Jabotinsky's grave for a long moment, then saluted, turned smartly on his heel and left — a small, bespectacled figure in a dark suit, white shirt, with lightly starched collar, plain tie neatly knotted and black felt hat — the epitome of the respectability he had attained at last in the political life of his country."

A short time later, Begin took his place in the cabinet; he was a political outcast no longer.

On June 5, as artillery duels raged along Israel's

President Gamal Abdel Nasser of Egypt was the fiery self-appointed spokesman of the pan-Arab movement during the 1960s. His goal was to unify all the Arab nations of the Middle East under the leadership of Egypt to ensure the annihilation of the state of Israel.

An Israeli convoy on its way to the Sinai Peninsula passes Egyptian prisoners of war, 1967. Responding to Nasser's threats, Israel launched a lightning attack against Egypt, Syria, and Jordan. The Israeli military overwhelmed its enemies on all three fronts in just six days, occupying territory that more than quadrupled the size of Israel.

borders with Egypt and Syria, Israel attacked Egypt and destroyed nearly 300 of its warplanes. Superiority of the skies thus assured, Israel went on to capture the Sinai and the Gaza Strip (the narrow piece of land along the Mediterranean between Egypt and Israel that had been part of the Palestine mandate and an active Arab base since 1948). As the fighting spread to other fronts, Israeli forces had similar successes. They captured Syria's Golan Heights, from which Syria had for years shelled and harassed Israeli settlements in the valley below. They also captured Judea and Samaria — the West Bank of the Jordan River — and the eastern half of Jerusalem, including the Old City, from Jordan. (The capture of the Old City, where many of the most historic and sacred buildings of the Jews were located, was particularly significant for the Jews.) Jordan had attacked despite a statement from Israel saying it would only engage Jordan in hostilities if Jordan started them. Begin was instrumental in urging Dayan to hasten the IDF's attempts to seize Jerusalem before a cease-fire could be arranged.

In just six days, in what history would call the Six-Day War, an outnumbered Israel had overwhelmed the Arabs, posting one of the greatest military achievements in modern times. Begin, who had long dreamed of the day when Israel would control the lands of its biblical heritage, was pleased. He felt the country was secure. Others were not so sure. As journalist Amos Elon wrote, ". . . in the mouths of many Israelis the delicious flavor of success was tempered by the accompanying bitterness of futility and frustration. Triumph was mixed with terror; war had resolved some of Israel's immediate concerns, but military success had scarcely affected the need for peace and reconciliation with her Arab neighbors. . . [The war] deepened rather than allayed the Arab sense of outrage at the establishment and success of a state which, in their eyes, seemed a foreign intrusion. The war saved Israel from extinction, but it remained a beleaguered fortress state. Israel had more than quadrupled the territory under its control, but it had conquered more land and people than it knew what to do with."

Begin remained in the unity government for three years, first under Eshkol, who suffered a fatal heart attack in early 1969, and then under Golda Meir. Meir had been a leading Jewish activist since her teens; though affiliated throughout her career with Labor Zionism, she and Begin nonetheless established a smooth working relationship. As she took office, hostilities between Israel and Egypt had reached a new peak. The Egyptians, apparently unwilling to accept the fact of their devastating defeat in the Six-Day War, waged a war of attrition along the Suez frontier, marked by border skirmishes, guerrilla assaults, and artillery bombardments. Cease-fire negotiations and wider peace plans put forth by the United States and the United Nations presented the Meir government with a crisis. The main issue was whether Israel should agree to give up the lands it had taken in 1967 and withdraw to its pre-1967 borders as part of an overall peace settlement with the Arab nations.

Begin was against accepting any such stipulations. "During all those years in opposition," he said, "my party and I believed we had a right to all of the land of Israel, even when parts of it were not under our control. Do you really think that we can

> *We were granted our right to exist by the God of our fathers, at the glimmer of the dawn of human civilization nearly four thousand years ago. For that right, which has been sanctified in Jewish blood from generation to generation, we have paid a price unexampled in the annals of nations.*
> —MENACHEM BEGIN

now agree to support the opposite of what we believe?" Begin again found himself in the minority, and in August 1970 the Israeli government accepted the various proposals. Begin then took the Gahal alliance out of the government and was criticized for not supporting the government's attempts to negotiate for peace. Still, said Begin, "I swear to you that in all my life I have never been more at peace with myself and my conscience than I am at the present moment." The cease-fire went into effect, but because no peace agreement resulted, Israel remained in the occupied territories. Meanwhile, a movement to populate the areas with Israeli settlers began. Begin wholeheartedly supported the colonization movement.

Further trouble came on October 6, 1973, as Jews around the world observed Yom Kippur. Egypt and Syria launched a surprise attack on Israel. This newest Arab attack found Begin in synagogue, praying and observing the holy day's ritual fast. Since the onslaught by Syria and Egypt took Israel almost completely by surprise, the new nation suffered heavy losses early in the conflict. After receiving

**In 1969 Golda Meir, former
labor minister, became
prime minister of Israel. Although Meir had a long association with Ben-Gurion's
Labor party, Begin agreed to
remain in her National Unity
government.**

AP/WIDE WORLD PHOTOS

arms from the United States, Israel gradually managed to turn back the Arab forces, but not before coming perilously close to disaster. The high death toll — some 2,400 Israeli lives — the staggering cost — estimated at nearly $7.4 billion, about as much as Israel's projected gross national product for the year — shook Israelis to the core. Many expressed their discontent at the polls in December by deserting the Labor government for a new Begin-led coalition known as the *Likud* (Hebrew for unity). Formed by Begin just before the Yom Kippur War by the addition of a few right-wing parties to the Gahal alliance, the Likud featured Begin and two rising stars of Israeli politics—Ezer Weizman, the sabra nephew of Chaim Weizmann and the architect of Israel's air force, and Ariel Sharon, the forceful general who guided Israel's rout of Egyptian forces in the Sinai during the war. The Likud captured 39 seats, an impressive performance but not enough to replace the labor alignment, which won 51 seats. Still, Begin was just a handful of seats short of claiming the mantle of power.

Begin talks to the press about the future of his Gahal party in the Meir government, 1970. Begin, opposed to a U.S.-sponsored peace plan that called for Israel to relinquish all territory gained in the 1967 war, pulled his party out of the National Unity government when Meir accepted the proposal.

9

The Reins of Power, the Pain of Peace

As Israelis went to the polls on May 17, 1977, they were asked by those who stood for office to choose between distinct visions for the future. The Labor alignment, at that point the only government Israel had ever known, was in disarray, wracked by scandals and thought by many to be running an unresponsive bureaucracy. Inflation had skyrocketed. The economy required massive infusions of aid from the United States. Memories of the Yom Kippur War remained fresh, and many people deeply resented the Labor establishment for what had happened. Still, none of the country's political analysts predicted a Likud victory, for in March 1974 Begin had suffered a heart attack that called into question his ability to handle the rigors of office. So serious was his collapse that a friend of his later commented, "Menachem was only a few heartbeats away from death."

But Ezer Weizman, given charge of the Likud effort, ran a clever campaign. He succeeded in transforming Begin's image, as one writer put it, "from rambunctious rebel to solid statesman." There was no questioning Begin's patriotism. Begin was also portrayed as an "incorruptible" leader, in obvious contrast to the Labor government politicians. Begin's longstanding position against giving up the

> *If the Likud is asked to form a government, then its first concern will be to prevent war.*
> —MENACHEM BEGIN
> on the Likud party
> platform

Prime Minister Begin on his historic visit to Cairo, Egypt, in 1979. His willingness to hold talks with Egypt seemed inconsistent. He had brought his new *Likud* party to power on a conservative, nationalist — some thought extremist — platform that appeared to preclude any compromise with Israel's Arab neighbors.

occupied territories won him support from the country's religious elements, many of whom were moving into those areas, and his generally hawkish (militant and hard-line) attitudes won him a large following from Jews who had fled to Israel from Arabic-speaking countries, primarily Morocco, Algeria, Egypt, Iraq, and Syria.

These Jews are generally known as the *Sephardim*, whereas Jews of central or eastern European origin are known as *Ashkenazim*. The Ashkenazim were in the forefront of the Zionist movement and generally backed the Labor party. The Sephardim were discriminated against by the more sophisticated Ashkenazim in matters of employment, education, and housing.

Begin had long been the champion of the Sephardim. Indeed, Herut called itself the party of the "poor, the suffering, and the oppressed." The Sephardim also identified more readily with Begin's ideas of Jewish strength and his hard-line stance toward the Arabs, under whose persecution they had lived for many years. (Begin also received some Ashkenazi support because he was a Polish Jew.)

The combined result of Labor's decline and Likud's improving fortunes was a stunning upset in Begin's favor. Commentators likened what happened to an "earthquake," a "deluge," and an "electoral storm." The Likud captured 43 seats to Labor's 32 seats.

The first signs of victory had been difficult to believe. Israel's leading newscaster, who had come on the air at 11 P.M. on that memorable evening, just. as the polls were closing across the country, was unable to disguise his astonishment at what he was about to report. His famous smile was completely absent as he reported that, based on a television sampling, Menachem Begin would be the next head of the Israeli government.

Begin himself, sitting quietly in front of his TV set in his small Tel Aviv apartment, reacted quietly and cautiously to the news and simply sat stirring the cup of tea that had become his trademark. Not for two more hours did he finally decide that the incredible victory was truly his and set off for Likud headquarters.

Defense Minister Ezer Weizmann (left) and Foreign Minister Moshe Dayan emerge from a cabinet meeting, 1978. In the previous year's national election, Weizmann ran the highly successful Likud campaign that presented Begin as a patriotic, incorruptible statesman.

A huge crowd was waiting to congratulate him and share in the precious triumph. He understood what the people were feeling, for when a policeman tried to force them aside in order to let him pass through, Begin told the officer to leave everyone as they were.

When he finally reached the hall upstairs, his thoughts were with his people still — this time with all the colleagues, friends, and close associates who had helped him over the years in so many significant struggles. Begin refused to talk into the reporters' microphones until he had spoken personally with each of them. When a persistent television commentator asked Begin whether the moment was the biggest of his life, he immediately replied, "Oh, no! There were bigger in the underground, in the war for Israel's independence."

The following month Menachem Begin was installed as prime minister, leading a 63-seat coalition government in the Knesset. Joining him were the religious parties and Moshe Dayan, who made a startling defection from Labor ranks to become Begin's foreign minister. Ezer Weizman became the new minister of defense. In October a 15-seat block of representatives joined the Likud coalition, giving Begin a 78-seat mandate to rule. The first government transfer in Israel's history was met with dis-

Jewish history in Israel came to a full stop when Ben-Gurion retired from politics and only resumed when I became prime minister.
—MENACHEM BEGIN

may abroad because of Begin's image as an extremist. Nonetheless, Begin promised good will and said that a dramatic overture for peace would be made during his administration.

The overture came, but it was not made by Begin. On November 9, 1977, President Anwar Sadat of Egypt made a momentous statement as he addressed his country's parliament: "Israel will be stunned to hear me tell you that I am ready to go to their home, to the Knesset itself, to argue with them, in order to prevent one Egyptian soldier from being wounded. Members of the People's assembly, we have no time to waste." Begin's reply was given through an American intermediary, for Israel and Egypt were still formally at war and had no diplomatic relations. Begin invited Sadat to come to Jerusalem. "May I assure you, Mr. President," the message said, "that the parliament, the government, and the people of Israel will receive you with respect and cordiality." Thus was set in motion the historic face-to-face encounters and negotiations between Israel and Egypt that led to the first peace treaty between Israel and one of its Arab neighbors.

Just days after Anwar Sadat's historic address, his plane landed at Israel's Ben-Gurion Airport. Greeting him were his wartime enemies of just four years earlier. To Golda Meir, prime minister during the Yom Kippur War, Sadat said, "Madame, I have been waiting to meet you for a long time." To Ariel Sharon, who had chased Egyptian forces back across the Suez, he said, "I wanted to catch you there." Sharon replied, "I'm glad to meet you here instead." To General Mordechai Gur, who warned the nation that Sadat might be using his visit as a ruse to start a war, he said, "I wasn't bluffing."

Sadat was greeted joyously wherever he went. Throughout his triumphant visit, during which he prayed at the el-Aksa Mosque and visited Yad Vashem, the Holocaust memorial and museum, Sadat delighted Israelis with his intelligence and candor. To most it was a dream come true, yet all Israelis also knew that the trip and the forces it set in motion were loaded with risk.

Sadat's gamble lay primarily in his breaking with

the Arab refusal to recognize Israel's right to exist. Many Arabs vehemently opposed Sadat's peace overtures. The Palestinians — those Arabs who had been displaced as a result of the establishment of the state of Israel — regarded Sadat's actions as a betrayal. They continued to press their claims for a homeland, often through terrorist activities sponsored by the Palestine Liberation Organization (PLO). There was a real possibility that Sadat would be assassinated. Sadat insisted that he was acting on behalf of all Arabs and that he was not trying to conclude a separate peace, as many of his critics charged. He promised to press the Arabs' case for Jerusalem and the occupied territories.

The risk for Begin lay in being forced, for the sake of peace, to withdraw from the occupied territories. The two leaders' addresses before the Knesset gave an indication of how difficult the approaching negotiations would be.

Sadat's performance was impressive. In sincere tones he said the words Israelis had waited a very long time to hear from an Arab leader: "We agree to live with you in peace and justice. Israel has become an accomplished fact, recognized by the whole world and the superpowers. We welcome you to live among us in peace and security." Sadat then voiced the Arabs' demand that all lands occupied by Israel in 1967 be returned. The challenge for peace had been issued.

Begin's response was less compelling. He restated many old positions, leading some people to fear that Sadat, for all his vision and trouble, would be going home "empty-handed." It was clear that Begin had found it hard to fashion a suitable reply to Sadat. Nonetheless, that was the task put before him and his country. As Sadat returned home, Israel's leaders knew that if they did not capitalize on the momentum toward peace created by Sadat's historic gesture, the occasion might never come again.

Begin visited the Egyptian city of Ismailia in late December. He and his entourage, remembering the flag-waving crowds that had greeted the Egyptian president on his entry to Jerusalem, were startled by the absence of any such festivities in Egypt. Be-

In Jerusalem, Sadat receives a welcoming gift from former prime minister Golda Meir. The two had been bitter enemies in the bloody 1973 Yom Kippur War, when Egypt and Syria had nearly defeated Israel in a surprise attack launched on the sacred Jewish high holiday.

gin presented a detailed peace plan, but he and Sadat made no headway at all, stalled as they were over the issue of the disputed territories. Moshe Dayan later described the alarm he had felt at this point: "I was deeply concerned about the price Egypt was determined to exact from us — total evacuation from Sinai; a commitment to withdraw completely from the West Bank and Golan; the rise of a Palestinian state. I sensed that there was a deep feeling behind these words: they were not mere lip-service. And I suspected that Israel would indeed be faced by the grim alternative of having to make heavy concessions or achieving no peace treaty with Egypt."

Over the next eight months, Begin was portrayed by the foreign press as an intransigent "obstacle" to peace for not being more flexible about the occupied territories. The two sides made little progress, and the excitement and optimism that had followed Sadat's visit gave way to doubt. In the end, it was the intensive involvement of U.S. president Jimmy Carter that salvaged the last remains of Egyptian-Israeli goodwill and paved the way for a historic peace treaty.

Carter, elected in 1976, had on many occasions voiced his desire to help bring about a comprehensive peace settlement in the Middle East. Some of his pronouncements, however, especially those calling for a Palestinian "homeland" and for Israeli flexibility over the West Bank, had led many Israelis to consider him too close to the Arab camp. In particular, they feared that because America was Israel's most important foreign ally, Israel would be forced to accept an agreement that would not take into account the country's security needs.

Carter and Begin had met the previous July and established a cordial relationship. Carter had stressed his continued willingness to supply Israel with generous military and economic aid. Still, he had found reason to write in the spring of 1978 that "My guess is that he [Begin] will not take the necessary steps to bring peace to Israel." Carter then went out on an unprecedented diplomatic limb by bringing Begin, Sadat, and their respective negotiating teams to the Camp David presidential retreat in Maryland in September for several days of talks.

"[We] worked day and night," Begin told the press conference that followed the historic summit meeting. "We used to go to bed at Camp David between 3:00 and 4:00 in the morning, arise. . . at 5:00 or 6:00 and continue working." At the end of 13 such days, Begin, Sadat, and Carter emerged with two documents: one that was to serve as the framework for an overall Middle East peace and another that was to be the framework for a separate Egypt-Israel peace treaty. "Peace now celebrates victory for the nations of Egypt and Israel and for all mankind," said Begin. The happy conclusion had been hard in coming. As Carter said after the exhausting negotiations, no one had expected "thirteen intense and discouraging days, with success in prospect only during the final hours."

Carter reported that Sadat and Begin each drove a hard bargain. "All restraint was gone," he wrote. "Their faces were flushed and the niceties of diplomatic language and protocol were stripped away.

> *The Arabs have so many countries, and we have only one. . . . I can't understand why they insist that this is their land.*
> —MENACHEM BEGIN
> on the claims of the Palestinians

In front of U.S. president Jimmy Carter, Begin and Sadat embrace after signing the 1978 agreement for peace negotiations between Israel and Egypt. The euphoria of the moment, however, was short lived, as both sides refused to compromise on certain critical issues.

They had almost forgotten that I was there." At one point Carter had to block the door of the cabin to keep a frustrated Sadat from walking out on the talks. Finally, with the creative input of presidential aides and a painstaking attention to detail on the part of Carter, formulas were reached, appropriate language was agreed upon, and the foundations for peace were laid. Sadat and Begin, who had last seen each other on day three of the talks, came together on day thirteen and promised to conclude a treaty within three months.

The irony for Begin upon his return to Israel was that some people thought he had made too many concessions. Still, Begin won Knesset approval for the accords. In October 1978 he and Sadat were awarded the Nobel Peace Prize.

The two then hardened their positions. Begin accelerated settlement on the West Bank in the apparent hope that, come the day when withdrawal was to occur, these "facts on the ground" might prevent the Israeli departure. The leader also defined more narrowly what he meant by the "autonomy" the Camp David accords would grant to the West Bank Palestinians living under Israeli rule. Sadat, for his part, sought to link the overall accords more closely with the fate of the Palestinians, in reaction to intense Arab opposition to the entire process and their charge that he had sold out the Palestinian cause. On March 1 Begin pronounced the peace talks to be "in a state of deep crisis."

Carter embarked on a week of shuttle diplomacy between Cairo and Jerusalem. As with the talks at Camp David, his efforts frequently came close to failure. On March 13 he secured final guarantees from Begin and Sadat, and two weeks later they were in Washington together, where they signed the peace treaty amid great fanfare.

The treaty provided for a three-stage Israeli withdrawal from the Sinai Peninsula. UN peacekeeping forces would be stationed along the Israel-Egypt border. Israeli ships would be free to pass through the Suez Canal, the Straight of Tiran, and the Gulf of Agalon, and Israel would have the right to purchase oil, under normal commercial terms, from the Sinai

A 1981 demonstration in support of Begin and the Likud party. Despite the compromises forced by the peace treaty, Begin continued to receive backing from his traditional supporters, the *Sephardim*, or immigrant Jews from Arab lands, who generally opposed giving in to Arab demands.

fields. Full diplomatic relations and economic and cultural ties between the two nations were established. In addition, a month after the treaty was ratified by the two countries' parliaments, negotiations were to begin on Palestinian autonomy in the West Bank and Gaza. Upon the successful completion of these talks, Israeli rule in these territories was to end. Some of Israel's armed forces were to remain in specific "security locations" as determined by the negotiators.

Unaffected by the Camp David treaty was the status of Jerusalem and the Golan Heights, and trouble was sure to accompany any Israeli retreat from the West Bank. But these were secondary considerations, at least for the moment. What most observers at the time focused on was that the rift between Egypt and Israel had been closed. Thirty years of war were over. Begin the warrior had brought peace to Israel.

10

Final Acts

The immediate effect of the Camp David treaty was not peace but turmoil. First of all, the other Arab nations severed diplomatic, financial, and economic ties with Egypt. Begin caused Egypt further distress by promptly stating three "nevers" about the treaty: Jerusalem would never again be a divided city, a Palestinian state would never be established on the West Bank, and Israel would never return to its pre-1967 borders. The remarks seemed at odds with the spirit of the treaty, but Begin kept his word and secured Knesset approval for the documents (the Egyptian parliament ratified them as well). Israel completed the first stage of its Sinai evacuation in April.

Three years later, on April 25, 1982, the withdrawal was complete. In the meantime much had happened to change the nature of the peace the Israelis had hoped for. Sadat had been assassinated in October of 1981 by Muslim fundamentalists opposed to his dealings with Israel, the United States, and other Western countries. The negotiations over Palestinian autonomy had not progressed. Begin was said to see the return of the Sinai as license to keep the West Bank. With Egypt in isolation and Israel apparently unwilling to budge on the occupied territories, the two countries settled into what has come to be known as a "cold peace." The borders

Begin combined something you don't often find in politicians, a very clear sense of what he wanted to do [and] a strict sense of what the political realities were and how you have to deal with them.
—WILLIAM QUANDT
former member, U.S.
National Security
Council

Begin is greeted by a Hebrew welcome and a strong political sentiment on a visit to the United States in November 1982. During his last years in office Begin came under increasing attack for his failure to follow through on the peace initiative and for his inability to curb rampant inflation at home.

UPI/BETTMANN NEWSPHOTOS

UPI/BETTMANN NEWSPHOTOS

The town of El Arish, captured by Israel in the 1967 Six-Day War, returns to Egyptian control, May 1979. In accordance with the treaty, Begin withdrew all Israeli troops from the occupied Sinai by 1982. Negotiations on the status of the West Bank and the Palestinians, however, were never seriously undertaken.

remain open, flags fly in the two capitals, but there is only a smattering of contact.

Begin's stand on the Palestinian issue, and the increasingly troubled Israeli economy (inflation in 1980 was 132.9 percent) led to doubts that he would be able to win reelection in 1981. His Likud coalition was struggling, reeling from the resignations of Dayan, Weizmann (who accused Begin of losing his faith in peace) and two finance ministers in quick succession. His physical condition was said to be deteriorating as well: Begin reportedly was subject to wild swings of energy and fatigue. Public opinion polls showed him behind Shimon Peres, who headed the Labor alignment's electoral slate.

Begin, however, pulled off an astounding political turnaround. He benefited from the voters' lack of confidence that Labor could cure Israel's economic problems and from large preelection tax cuts on desirable consumer goods such as automobiles and television sets. He also revived physically and campaigned across the country to cheers of "Begin, King of Israel." But violence marred many of his political rallies, and he was charged with fanning the flames of the Ashkenazim-Sephardim split. Said one Labor leader: "There is an atmosphere of social incitement

Menachem Begin must be the only party leader in the democratic world to have lost eight consecutive elections and lived to win a ninth and tenth.

—ERIC SILVER
British journalist, on
Begin's political career

and nationalist incitement. Experience teaches us that when these two elements are combined it always leads to fascism. Begin is appealing to the lowest section of the population."

The Sephardim resented such comments as indicative of a strong bias against them. They also continued, for the most part, to back Begin's foreign policy and his definition of security needs. When an Israeli bomber raid destroyed a nuclear reactor under construction in Iraq on June 7, 1981, he won new supporters across ethnic lines. The air raid, which had been planned and approved in late 1980, was designed to prevent Iraq from developing nuclear weapons that Begin believed would be used

Begin, the Polish Jew, divided the country between east and west as it had never been divided before.
—ERIC SILVER
British journalist

AP/WIDE WORLD PHOTOS

Israeli soldiers command a hilltop overlooking West Beirut, July 1982. The June invasion of Lebanon, a move intended to rout the Palestine Liberation Organization from its bases there, became bogged down in Lebanese internal politics and ended up a disaster for the Begin government.

Defense Minister Ariel Sharon oversaw the invasion of Lebanon. The Israeli army was blamed for the horrifying massacre in September 1982 of innocent civilians at Palestinian refugee camps outside of Beirut. The incident sparked a raging debate in Israel over its policy in Lebanon.

against Israel. As he said, "Where is the country that would tolerate such a danger? There won't be another Holocaust in the history of the Jewish people. Never again."

Likud had passed Labor in public opinion polls before the raid, but the success of the mission surely helped its electoral chances. On June 30 Begin was reelected prime minister, winning 48 seats to Labor's 47 in the closest election in Israeli history. Once again, Begin formed a governing coalition with the religious parties and other right-wing supporters.

On June 6, 1982, Israel launched a large-scale invasion of Lebanon. The attack was aimed at driving the PLO from Lebanon, where it had established bases and camps and continued its guerrilla war against Israel. Begin wanted to push the PLO away from Israel's border in order to prevent it from bombarding northern Israel. Defense Minister Ariel Sharon said after the initial attack that "Operation Peace for Galilee," as it was named, would be over in 48 hours. Instead it became a protracted affair, the most divisive war in Israel's history, as the Israelis became enmeshed in the turbulent politics and fierce factional fighting that had divided Lebanon since the early 1970s. It led to widespread international condemnation of Israel and fierce criticism of the war within Israel. Some commentators believe it was the criticism he received on Lebanon that brought about the eventual resignation of Menachem Begin.

The PLO, under the leadership of Yasir Arafat, was, in the words of a 1974 proclamation by the Arab League (an association of Arab states; Egypt was expelled after the peace treaty with Israel), the "sole legitimate representative of the Palestinian people." Since the 1960s the PLO has waged a multifront struggle for Palestinian rights: a worldwide propaganda campaign to publicize its cause; a service campaign to improve the daily lives of its people through the establishment of schools, hospitals, and the like; and a military campaign against Israel characterized by attacks against civilian Jews in Israel and abroad, all the while rejecting any form of peaceful diplomacy. Among its more notorious efforts have been the killing of 11 Israeli athletes at the 1972 Olympic Games in Munich, West Germany; an attack on a school in northern Israel in which lives were lost; and a tour-bus hijacking in which 32 people were killed.

The PLO had taken root in Lebanon after its defeat in 1970 in a civil war in Jordan, where it had threatened the rule of King Hussein. The virtual anarchy in Lebanon, where a civil war had raged since 1975, allowed the PLO to carve out a "state within a state." Begin wanted to destroy this structure.

Israeli troops had no problem pushing the PLO back beyond artillery range of Israeli territory. In fact, much of the local Lebanese population, which had hated the Palestinian presence, joyously greeted the Israelis as liberators. When the IDF pushed on to the Lebanese capital, Beirut, in the process revealing a grander design to its Lebanon invasion, an international outcry resulted. Israel laid siege to the city, bombarding it from air, land, and sea. It became clear that the operation was intended not only to drive the PLO from the Israeli border, as

In February 1983 angry demonstrators called for the resignation of Sharon after a government panel assigned substantial blame to him for the massacres in Lebanon. Reaction to the commission's report was sharply divided throughout Israel.

UPI/BETTMANN NEWSPHOTOS

initially stated, but to eradicate it entirely. Israel did not relax its grip on Beirut until thousands of trapped PLO fighters were evacuated and sent to eight Arab nations. Most Israelis supported the government to that point, though some dissent was heard about the operation having gone too far.

The invasion soon turned sour. Israel had hoped that the election in August of its Christian ally, Bashir Gemayel, as Lebanon's president would cement a de facto peace between Israel and Lebanon. (Much of the tension and violence in Lebanon was due to hostility between the country's Christian and Muslim populations. The Muslims, though a majority within Lebanon, believed that the Christians dominated the country both politically and economically. The PLO presence exacerbated these tensions.) In mid-September Gemayel was assassinated by Muslims. Israeli troops then occupied Beirut, ostensibly to keep order. Seeking to root out any PLO fighters who might have evaded the evacuation by hiding in the city's Palestinian refugee camps, Lebanese Christian soldiers massacred hundreds of Palestinian men, women, and children in the camps.

Israel was blamed for the carnage. It was said that

A tour group visits a peaceful Israeli development in the Golan Heights, 1980. One of the most complex issues of a Mideast peace settlement centers around Israeli colonization of occupied territories.

Israel should have foreseen the possibility of a massacre — nothing new to Lebanese fighting — and prevented it from occurring. It was also alleged that Israeli troops had apparently failed to step in even after they learned that the Christians had begun the slaughter. Begin responded to these charges by saying that the world had brought a "blood libel" against Israel.

Demonstrations in Israel — one protest rally drew some 400,000 people, roughly 10 percent of Israel's population — and other pressures forced Begin to appoint a commission of inquiry. That panel released its report in February 1982. It placed substantial blame on Defense Minister Ariel Sharon for his role in the affair and said of Begin that "The Prime Minister's lack of involvement in the entire matter casts on him a certain degree of responsibility."

In the meantime, Israel had settled into a military occupation of southern Lebanon. In contrast to its determination to hold on to the West Bank, how-

Thousands of marchers organized by _Gush Emunim_ ("Bloc of the Faithful"), a militant, right-wing group, demonstrate in support of the annexation of the West Bank, 1976. The region has attracted intensely nationalistic settlers who want to regain for Israel an area rich in Jewish biblical history. Begin maintained that the West Bank was critical to Israel's defense.

ever, Israel had no intentions of keeping the land; its intention was to stay until the situation was under control. Israeli casualties steadily mounted as the resentful Lebanese fought the occupation, and opposition within Israel to the entire Lebanon affair increased. Begin found himself under siege at home.

In the midst of this tumult came the death of Aliza Begin on November 13, 1982, after a prolonged illness associated with her chronic asthma. Begin plunged into deep grief. Over the next several months, it seemed, he lost his desire to govern. His appetite waned, he rarely appeared in public, and he became depressed and unfocused. On August 28, 1983, at the end of a cabinet meeting, he told his ministers, "I cannot go on." In September Herut chose Yitzhak Shamir, a one-time member of the Stern Gang, to replace Begin as prime minister. An era had ended.

In a family portrait from 1977 Begin holds one of his eight grandchildren as his wife, Aliza (top left), daughters Leah (right) and Hasia, and son-in-law Mati look on. Begin always saw his actions in terms of providing for the future generations of Israel a strong nation free from the threat of attack by its Arab neighbors.

Menachem Begin lives today in Jerusalem. He is visited on occasion by his family and confidants but remains, for the most part, a recluse. The state he helped found was made both more secure and more vulnerable by his actions. His peace treaty with Egypt defused the Arab threat on one frontier, but his support of West Bank colonization made the problem more volatile there. His policies created a stronger Israel, less vulnerable to Arab aggression, at the cost of an increasingly divided population.

Begin was followed by a succession of coalition and unity governments that lacked his vision and vigor. Some Israelis favored this state of affairs, preferring less ideology and more pragmatism. But others, even some Labor party members, have expressed a desire to see a person of Begin's stature —if not his politics—at the top again.

Prime Minister Begin, who grew a beard in the traditional sign of mourning, sits in the Knesset, 1982. After Aliza died in November of that year Begin withdrew from political life, leaving his successors to grapple with the many troubling issues that divide the Israeli people.

Further Reading

Aufderheide, Patricia. *Anwar Sadat.* New York: Chelsea House, 1986.

Begin, Menachem. *The Revolt.* London: W. H. Allen, 1983.

———. *White Nights: The Story of a Prisoner in Russia,* trans. by Katie Kaplan. New York: Harper & Row, 1977.

Elon, Amos. *The Israelis: Founders and Sons.* New York: Holt, Reinhart, and Winston, 1971.

Gervasi, Frank. *The Life and Times of Menahem Begin.* New York: G. P. Putnam's Sons, 1979.

Haber, Eitan. *Menachem Begin: The Legend and the Man,* trans. by Louis Williams. New York: Delacorte, 1978.

Hirschler, Gertrude, and Lester S. Eckman. *Menahem Begin.* New York: Shengold, 1979.

Silver, Eric. *Begin: The Haunted Prophet.* New York: Random House, 1984.

Vail, John J. *David Ben-Gurion.* New York: Chelsea House, 1987.

Chronology

Aug. 16, 1913	Born Menachem Begin in Brest-Litovsk
Nov. 2, 1917	Great Britain issues Balfour Declaration, expressing support for a Jewish homeland in Palestine
1928	Begin joins *Betar*, the militant Zionist youth movement founded by Vladimir Ze'ev Jabotinsky
1931	Enters University of Warsaw to study law
1939	British White Paper restricts Jewish immigration to Palestine Begin appointed Betar commissioner for Poland; marries Aliza Arnold
1939–45	Adolf Hitler implements his Final Solution, setting up concentration camps across Europe, where more than 6 million Jews are killed
1940–41	Begin imprisoned by Soviet authorities
1942	Arrives in Palestine as a private in the Polish army
Dec. 1943	Assumes command of the *Irgun Z'vai Leumi*, a Zionist military underground organization
Feb. 1944	The Irgun initiate a revolt against British rule in Palestine
Nov. 1944	British minister Lord Moyne assassinated
1945–46	Irgun and Haganah join forces to resist British occupation and immigration restrictions
July 22, 1946	The Irgun bombs the King David Hotel in Jerusalem
1947	Britain gives up its mandate; UN General Assembly votes for the partition of Palestine
May 14, 1948	State of Israel established
1948–49	Israeli War of Independence
June 1948	The supply ship *Altalena* is destroyed in a showdown between the Irgun and the provisional government
Jan. 1949	Begin elected to the Knesset, or Parliament, as head of the *Herut* party
1957	Publishes *White Nights*
1967–70	Serves as a cabinet minister in the coalition government
1973	Forms the *Likud* bloc, expanding his parliamentary support
May 1977	Likud wins general election; Begin becomes prime minister
Nov. 1977	Egyptian president Anwar el-Sadat visits Jerusalem
Sept. 1978	Begin, Sadat, and U.S. president Carter meet at Camp David
Oct. 1978	Begin and Sadat awarded Nobel Peace Prize
March 26, 1979	Begin and Sadat sign peace treaty between Israel and Egypt
June 7, 1981	Begin sends Israeli warplanes into Iraq to destroy a nuclear power plant under construction
June 1982	Israel invades Lebanon
Sept. 1983	Begin resigns

Index

Richard Amdur is a New York-based writer whose work has appeared in *The New York Times, Psychology Today, Cosmopolitan,* and many other publications. He lived for more than a year on a kibbutz in Israel.

Arthur M. Schlesinger, jr., taught history at Harvard for many years and is currently Albert Schweitzer Professor of the Humanities at City University of New York. He is the author of numerous highly praised works in American history and has twice been awarded the Pulitzer Prize. He served in the White House as special assistant to Presidents Kennedy and Johnson.